4 DVD COLLECTORS CENTENARY LIMITED EDITION

ON THE WESTERN FRONT
THE GREAT WAR 1914 - 1918

Written by Mike Lepine

Danann
BOOKS

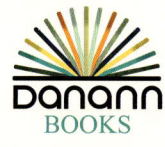

BOOKS

© Danann Publishing Ltd

First Published Danann Publishing Ltd 2014

CAT NO: UPE0226

Photography courtesy of Photoshot,

Book layout & design Darren Grice at **Ctrl-d**

Quality of original archive material may vary throughout the programme. DVD's are engineered to the highest possible standards.
Viewing experience will vary from player to player.

Made in EU.
ISBN: 978-0-9576909-1-2

CONTENTS

FOREWORD .... **page 4**

1914   **page 6**

SARAJEVO | THE GREAT EUROPEAN POWERS IN 1914 | ON THE BRINK | THE SCHLIEFFEN PLAN | BRITAIN ENTERS THE WAR | THE BRITISH EXPEDITIONARY FORCE IN 1914 | SOLDIERS OF THE DOMINION | THE RAPE OF BELGIUM | THE BATTLE OF THE FRONTIERS | MONS | THE FIRST TO DIE | KITCHENER'S MOB | THE FIRST BATTLE OF THE MARNE | THE 'RACE TO THE SEA' | THE FIRST BATTLE OF YPRES | THE TRENCHES | THE CHRISTMAS TRUCE

1915   **page 30**

AIR POWER | THE CHAMPAGNE OFFENSIVE | NEUVE CHAPELLE | THE SECOND BATTLE OF YPRES | ARTOIS AND VIMY RIDGE | LOOS AND CHAMPAGNE – THE 'BIG PUSH'.

1916   **page 48**

CONSCRIPTION | THE BATTLE OF VERDUN | PLANNING THE SOMME OFFENSIVE | THE SOMME – THE OPENING BARRAGE | THE FIRST DAY OF THE SOMME | THE SOMME OFFENSIVE | THE TANK

1917   **page 70**

SHELL SHOCK | RETREAT TO THE HINDENBURG LINE | AMERICA ENTERS THE WAR | THE GRAND SPRING OFFENSIVE | ARRAS AND VIMY RIDGE | THE NIVELLE OFFENSIVE THE FRENCH MUTINIES | THE FLANDERS OFFENSIVE | THE BATTLE OF CAMBRAI

1918   **page 90**

OPERATION MICHAEL | OPERATION GEORGETTE | THE BLUCHER YORCK OFFENSIVE | THE GNEISENAU OFFENSIVE | THE FAILURE OF KAISERSCHLACHT | THE SECOND BATTLE OF THE MARNE | AMIENS | THE '100 DAY OFFENSIVE' BEGINS | ASSAULTING THE HINDENBURG LINE | THE KIEL MUTINY | THE ROAD TO PEACE | THE DYING DAYS

1919   **page 110**

VERSAILLES AND BEYOND

FOREWORD

The centenary of the start of the Great War was bound to lead to reinterpretations of the events of 1914-18. However, it's far from the first time. The events and dates of history may be largely fixed, but how we see them and judge them is quite another matter.

Those present day advocates of what's becoming known as the 'Blackadder' view of the Great War - that it was nothing more than four years of senseless carnage on an unimaginable scale – might be surprised to learn that the War was not always seen this way.

In the decade following the Great War, those in Britain largely thought of it as a terrible struggle but one that was absolutely necessary. It wasn't until the 1930s when, beset by depression, the nation really started to question the war. Now it was seen as pointless, because the war had ultimately done nothing to help Britain prosper. A decade later, with Britain in the thick of another conflict, the Great War became a 'good war' once again, one in which Britain had fought and prevailed against the bestial Germans.

The present predominating view of the war originates from a relatively new way of perceiving and teaching history. It was developed by Marxist thinking in the 1960s. This view of history hated everything about empires, euro centrism, capitalism, nationalism, patriotism, class differences, war and militarism. It started from the position that these were the world's greatest evils – and used the Great War as an example of all that was wrong with the Capitalist system. The viewpoint had an appeal, it was zealously promoted and today it prevails. At the same time, the work of the 'War Poets' – Owen, Sassoon et al – began to be taught in schools and gain attention as never before, until many thought that they spoke for their entire generation.

Now in recent times there have been attempts, mainly by the conservative right, to challenge that view of the Great War and to see in it positive examples of human behaviour and values. This new approach calls for a re-examination of everything we think we know about the War and to better understand it from the context of the time when it was fought, rather than through contemporary eyes and through the heavy blinkers of radical ideologies. **The truth as usual lies somewhere between the extremes.**

The Great War was a product of the tensions both between and within empires. Unscrupulous capitalists did make fortunes from the misery. The scale of the carnage that ensued was enormous. Offensives did go horribly wrong. Mistakes were made with staggering loss of life as a consequence: 30,000 casualties here, 60,000 casualties there. A million casualties. These are figures that probably can't ever be adequately comprehended. As Josef Stalin is alleged to have said, 'One death is a tragedy. A million deaths is a statistic.'

However, to apportion equal blame to all nations is to apply cultural and moral equivalence to a frankly ignorant degree. All nations were not equally to blame. Some were eager for war. Others were not. From the British perspective, the nation ostensibly went to war because of its treaty obligations towards Belgium. However its leaders also knew – and to a large extent the ordinary people understood – that Britain could not tolerate a Western Europe dominated by a militaristic Germany. Given the resources in captured lands, industries and enslaved people, it would directly threaten Britain and its Empire. Germany would always envy what Britain had, and see the ultimate solution as the invasion of Britain. As Germany militarised and moved in 1914, Britain simply had no choice.

From a modern perspective, we cannot adequately understand the depths of patriotism and the sense of duty that British people of all classes felt in 1914. Now that notions like patriotism are useless to them, our betters have seen fit to try to wipe them from contemporary thinking. They served. They sacrificed - and they saw it as their duty. It may be a long way to Tipperary – but it's an even longer way to 1914. When it comes to matters of class, of course there were differences between the officers and the ranks - but the sons of earls and merchant bankers bled and died on the wire next to the

children of miners and mill workers. Prime Minister Asquith's eldest son Raymond died on the Somme.

It's true that the commanders sent millions to their deaths, but they were fighting what was almost an unwinnable war. Once the stalemate of the trenches had set in, the battlefield always favoured the defenders. No-one could move. Faced with this, the commanders were often forced to settle for a ghastly war of attrition. Perhaps they shouldn't have, but they did. At the same time, new technology was changing the battlefield and commanders had to develop fresh ways of co-ordinating artillery, men, tanks and aircraft. It took time. These were men trained in the age of cavalry. The sheer industrial scale of offensives also set new problems in command, communications and logistics. Napoleon could observe the battle of Waterloo with a spy glass. Clashes during the Great War could take place over tens or even hundreds of square miles. Commanders might win a battle, only to lose it again because they did not know they had won and failed to take the appropriate action. Indeed, it happened time and again.

Could the Great War have been avoided? Probably not. The whole continent was a powder keg or tinderbox or whichever cliché you want to use. All it took was Austro-Hungary moving against Serbia to start the war, egged on by a frankly indecently excited Germany. If it hadn't been that, it would have doubtless been something else very soon after.

From a British perspective, when war broke out we felt seriously threatened and sought to defend ourselves. We did not seek the war. We did not start the war. If you believe in peace at any price and that it is always better to appease than oppose, then the First World War will always be a 'wrong war'. If you believe that it is the right thing to do to stand against those who would harm you and innocent others, you may see something quite different in the Great War.

Mike Lepine - Leicestershire. 2014

'Europe today is a powder keg...
Some damned foolish thing in the Balkans will set it off.'
Otto von Bismarck, 1878

Archduke Franz Ferdinand in Sarajevo, June 1914.

Serbien muss sterbien! ("Serbia must die!"), Austrian propaganda artwork, after the assassination of Franz Ferdinand in 1914. Image showing the Austrian hand crushing a Serb terrorist.

Nedeljko Cabrinovic, a member of the Young Bosnia movement, and one of the seven who intended to assassinate Franz Ferdinand.

SARAJEVO

On the morning of Sunday, 28th June 1914, Archduke Franz Ferdinand and his wife Sophie stepped down from their train into bright sunshine in the Bosnian city of Sarajevo and then embarked in a convoy of six cars en route to the town hall.

Ferdinand was the heir apparent to the throne of the Austro-Hungarian Empire. Those who knew him didn't think much of him. He was uncharismatic, strange, uncommunicative, untroubled by academic achievement and rumoured to be partially insane thanks to inbreeding. He spent his days hunting animals around the world, and had reached a tally of 300,000 beasts according to his diaries. His secondary hobby was interior design. He had also married beneath him – Sophie was a lady-in-waiting – and that alone had caused a constitutional crisis that shook the already fragile empire. This was perhaps his one saving grace. He truly loved his wife. Today – 28th June – was their 14th wedding anniversary. Back in the heart of empire, Sophie was refused permission to sit in the same royal carriage as her husband. Out here on the periphery, they were free to sit together in the same car and enjoy their anniversary. Unfortunately, Sunday June 28th was not just their anniversary. It was also Serbian National Day.

Lying in wait for the Archduke in Sarajevo that morning was a gang of well-prepared men armed with pistols and explosives. They were Serbian nationalists, almost certainly secretly supported by the Serbian state. Bosnia was an Austro-Hungarian protectorate and the nationalists wanted to see it free of the empire to be part of a greater Slavic nation to be called Yugoslavia.

Ferdinand's route to the town hall was well known and three bombers were placed along the route. The first two failed to act and the motorcade passed by unscathed. The third nationalist, Nedeljko Cabrinovic, threw his bomb but it bounced off the rear of Ferdinand's car and exploded under the car behind, injuring its occupants and some 15 spectators. Fearful of capture, Cabrinovic swallowed a cyanide capsule. It didn't work. Hastily, he threw himself into the nearby Miljacka River to drown – only to discover it was just 5 inches deep at that point. He sat there helpless as an angry crowd set about beating him – and had to be rescued by police as the Archduke's motorcade sped away.

Once at the town hall, Ferdinand gave his pre-arranged speech (with a few added sarcastic comments about the assassination attempt) and then insisted on going to hospital to visit the wounded. Another motorcade was hastily assembled and set off again. By sheer bad luck, it would pass straight by another member of the nationalist gang, 19-year-old Gavrilo Princip, who was sitting at a table in a street café. He seized the opportunity, pulled his pistol and strode across the street to Ferdinand's car, opening fire from a distance of five feet. His first shot hit the Archduke in the throat. He then shot Sophie in the stomach. She was pregnant. Ferdinand's driver took the stricken couple out of danger and headed to the governor's residence, with the Archduke clinging to his wife and begging her not to die. It was already too late. The Archduke himself succumbed to his wound ten minutes after arriving at the residence.

When news of the assassination spread, anti-Serb riots broke out not just in Sarajevo but throughout the Austro-Hungarian Empire. Austria-Hungary consulted their closest Allies, the Germans, about what they should do. The Kaiser, in a particularly bad mood that day, agreed with the Austro-Hungarian assessment: this was the ideal opportunity to fight a small central European war and crush Serbia once and for all. The Kaiser announced,' *The Serbs must be disposed of – and soon'*. His powerful and influential Military Chief of Staff, Helmuth von Moltke, joined in the sabre rattling, agreeing that it should be *'War! And the sooner the better!'*

Armed with this 'blank cheque' from the Germans, the Austro-Hungarians made strong threats against Serbia. Unable to placate the empire, Serbia mobilised its army, buoyed up by promises of support from its closest ally, Russia. A small and seeming inconsequential exchange of fire on the Danube led to a formal declaration of war on Serbia by Austria-Hungary on 28th July and it partly mobilised its troops. This obliged Russia and France to mobilise their armies in response – and Germany followed.

Early portrait of Archduke Franz Ferdinand.

Gavrilo Princip another member of the Young Bosnia movement who fired the fatal shot that killed Franz Ferdinand.

Hanging of Serbs in Trebinje 1914.

Wilhelm II. Emperor of Germany.

The war was on.

One last terrible irony is that, had he lived, Ferdinand could well have been a great peacemaker. For all his faults, he wanted better treatment for all Slav peoples including the Serbs and had proposed that the Slavs become an equal third part of the Austro-Hungarian power structure. He also believed in making more reconciliatory and even friendly moves towards his traditional enemy Russia. He never lived to put his ideas into practice.

THE GREAT EUROPEAN POWERS IN 1914

GERMANY

Germany was only unified into one nation in 1871 and so came late to the great games of European power-broking and empire building. A youthful nation dominated by old militaristic Prussian attitudes, it was determined to catch up fast.

Its geographical location made it inherently paranoid, with the brutish might of Imperial Russia to its East and old enemies France to the West. Germany not only felt surrounded by its enemies. It also had a bad case of empire envy. The Germans utterly despised Belgium – but even tiny Belgium had a half way decent empire. As the 20th Century progressed, Germany had become an industrial powerhouse. However, it had next to no Empire to trade with. The Germans looked with envious eyes on the British Empire. They wanted it. Considerable resources were devoted to building the second most powerful fleet in the world – a direct threat to British maritime supremacy. This is not to suggest that Germany was spoiling for all-out war with Britain but having enough muscle might make Britain a little more amenable to German territorial ambitions. Germany also had another problem – its Kaiser. Kaiser Wilhelm II had a withered left arm and an English mother, both of which troubled him deeply. Insecure about both his identity and his manhood, he overcompensated with a love of grand uniforms, hanging out with military men and playing at soldiers.

A frightened little boy who loved to play tough, he was putty in the hands of the military elite who truly ran Germany.

GREAT BRITAIN

In the years immediately preceding the outbreak of World War One, Britannia not only ruled the waves but good portions of the world too. It was content, complacent, tough and stand-offish when it came to Europe. It had no real desires to cut itself a slice of the continent. It had vast lands overseas from which to trade and extract untold wealth. The old enemies the French were on reasonable speaking terms and most of the other great European empires seemed remote and irrelevant. There might be odd fights over colonial territories, but they were far away. The one European power Britain was truly wary of was Germany – with good reason.

In 1871, a book called 'The Battle of Dorking' was published. Written by George Chesney, it told the fantastical tale of Britain being invaded by an enemy nation which was Germany in all but name. Chesney, a military man, had seen just how efficient Germanic forces had been during the Franco-Prussian War of 1870-1 and was worried about their ability to conscript vast numbers of soldiers. His book provoked fierce debate in senior military and political services, leading to an invigoration of Britain's reserves. Paranoid or not, Chesney's fears were widely shared in influential quarters.

By the start of the 20th Century, Germany's army was far mightier than Britain's and its navy was expanding fast. German statements such as 'the trident must pass into our hands' was a direct threat to British supremacy at sea. In 1909, there were widespread reports of German Zeppelins making mysterious reconnaissance missions by night over the south and east of England – especially over military installations or dockyards. The reports proved to be false – Zeppelins could not yet safely traverse the North Sea – but the fear persisted.

FRANCE

At the start of 1914, there were still many in France who remembered their ignominious defeat in 1871 at the hands of the Prussians and their allies from the Germanic States. The successful invaders had annexed Alsace and Lorraine, two French

Portrait of King George V.

Portrait of Raymond Poincaré.

Early Portrait of Franz Joseph I of Austria.

Portrait of the Sultan of the Ottoman empire Mehmed V.

Portrait of Victor Emmanuel III of Italy.

Thomas Mann in 1900.

provinces rich in industry, coal and minerals and had been living off their wealth ever since. The French dearly wanted them back - and a cold slice of revenge too. However it was not enough to make them go to war, despite being a strong, powerful and successful nation with a large army and an empire of very real worth. War would be brought upon them.

AUSTRIA-HUNGARY

The Austro-Hungarian Empire was in decline. Ludicrouslygrand, enormously self-important and dangerously out-of-date, it could feel itself crumbling along with its emperor, the aging and almost senile Franz Joseph I. It comprised the nobility of Austria and Hungary, Germanics and Magyars: men from fairy-tale castles who were sick from centuries of inbreeding, hidebound by custom and convention and who had almost a uniquely poor grasp of changing political realities. Their empire consisted of a large chunk of the Balkans, which seemed to be perpetually in flames. Here were vast numbers of Slavic people, who the Germanics especially thought of as sub-human. Here too were Muslims, still hated many hundreds of years after they had attempted to conquer Europe, Here were nations like Serbia, awash with proto-fascistic ideas about race and nationalism and eager to torment and ultimately tear down the ailing empire on its doorstep. The Austro-Hungarian Empire was a multicultural hellhole, with no common dream to hold it together. The rulers were weak and their enemies fired with eagerness for a grand new day free of the imperial yoke.

RUSSIA

Russia too had eyes on the Balkans to its western fringes. It could see the way the wind was blowing. Austria-Hungary could not hope to remain a major power for very much longer – and when it finally fell, Russia intended to be first in line to pick up its vacated territories. Being a Slavic people at heart, the Russians were naturally predisposed to supporting the newly emerging Slavic power in the region – Serbia – and revelled in the way Serbia tormented and strained the Austro-Hungarians.

Imperial Russia had its problems too though. Things got done slowly there. It was grand but vastly inefficient.

A few enjoyed undreamed of riches while a vast peasant population suffered grotesque poverty and cruel oppression. The Russian imperial army was immense – but badly funded and equipped. It was an army more suited to an older age.

TURKEY

Like Austro-Hungary, Turkey too was an empire deep in decline. It too had once owned vast tracts of the Balkans and had fallen foul of the rising ethnic and nationalistic uprisings that had turned the region into one vast powder keg over the past fifty years in particular. Attempts at appeasing Christians who wanted their lands free of Islamic rule only served to encourage them further. As successful Slav nationalist movements drove increasing numbers of Muslims back into the heart of Islamic Turkey for safety, their influence further waned. Christian nationalism wasn't the only problem. The Ottoman rulers faced fierce opposition from their Kurdish subjects, fellow Moslems to a man. The Empire was coming apart – fast.

ITALY

Italy was another relatively new power, only unified in 1871. Nominally, it had an alliance with the Central European Powers and should have joined with Germany and Austro-Hungary when war broke. It didn't. It neither felt it had to fight to survive nor fight to gain new territory. It was also more than a little wary of Royal Navy power in the Mediterranean, being a country with so much coastline. Instead it remained neutral until 15th April 1915, when it finally decided to join the Allies in exchange for the promise of choice chunks of Austrian territory after victory.

ON THE BRINK

'The German soul will emerge stronger, prouder, freer, happier from (war)'
Thomas Mann

Austro-Hungary would not have invaded Serbia without the promised support of Kaiser Wilhelm and Germany. Serbia would not have provoked Austro-Hungary

A Berlin crowd listens as a German officer reads the Kaiser's order for mobilisation on **1st August 1914.**

Helmuth Johann Ludwig von Moltke.

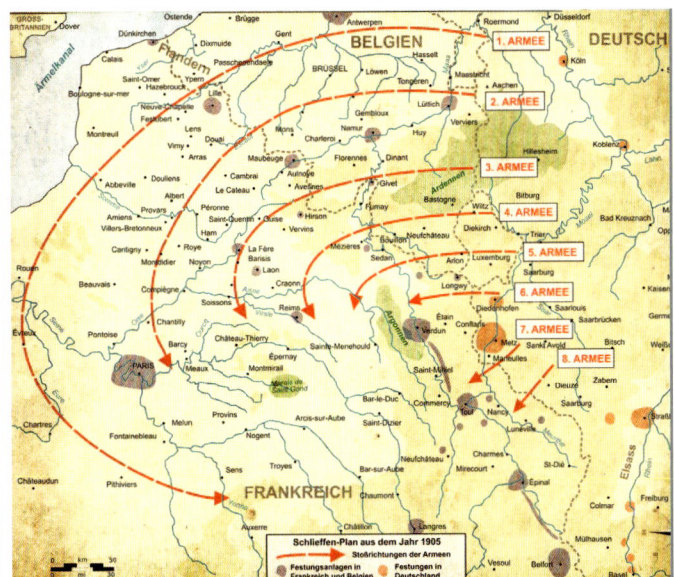

German Map of the Schlieffen Plan of 1905.

IT IS FAR BETTER TO FACE THE BULLETS THAN TO BE KILLED AT HOME BY A BOMB

JOIN THE ARMY AT ONCE & HELP TO STOP AN AIR RAID

GOD SAVE THE KING

British WW I poster.

so mightily had the Czar not given it a direct declaration of support. Once Austro-Hungary was at war and Russia was militarising, Germany had no choice but to support its brother Germans in Austria and respond to the threat of a militarised Russia on its eastern borders. France then had to mobilise to support Russia against the German threat, thanks to an alliance dating back to 1894. In high places, it was what some had dreamed of. In others, it was precisely what they had dreaded. There was still a chance to pull back from the brink, still a chance for last minute peace talks and for cooler heads to prevail.

Except there was a problem. Germany had a plan to win the war – but it meant shooting first and talking later.

THE SCHLIEFFEN PLAN

'Paris for lunch, dinner in St Petersburg!'
Kaiser Wilhelm II

At the start of the war, Germany put 'The Schlieffen Plan' into immediate effect.

Germany had long feared having to fight a war on a two fronts – with the grand imperial power of Russia to its East and traditional enemies France to its West. To counteract this threat, The Schlieffen Plan was devised in 1905 by Count Alfred von Schlieffen (then the Chief of the Imperial German General Staff). The aim of the plan was to knock France out of the war as quickly as possible with a massive surprise attack. The full might of the German war machine could then be concentrated against the Russians. Rather than assault the formidable French network of fortified border positions, the German Army would bypass them by racing through Luxembourg and Belgium before sweeping south and then east to Paris, surrounding the city and forcing France to surrender. Leaving only a small occupying army behind, the bulk of the victorious German forces could then be sent quickly to the Russian Front by Railway.

It was estimated that Russia would need at least six weeks to mobilise properly, so Paris had to be surrounded within 31 days of war and the surrender of France secured in just 42 days. It was assumed that Belgium would offer little or no resistance and Britain would either remain neutral or be ineffective. (Bismarck had once joked that if the British Army dared to put foot on German soil, he would simply have the police arrest them). It was the tightest of timetables, with next to no margin for deviation or error.

Everything depended on speed. There would simply be no time for diplomacy, no time for peace talks. If Germany was going to win, it had to go to war immediately. So when the Chief of the German General Staff Helmuth von Moltke put the Schlieffen Plan into effect on 1st August 1914, the clock was ticking.

The threat to Luxembourg and Belgium was obvious – and immediate.

BRITAIN ENTERS THE WAR

Great Britain didn't enter the war in order to support either France or Russia. There were treaties -but nothing that obliged it to act. At the time, Britain was actually distrustful of Russia and there had been several clashes in the Far East when the Great Bear had threatened its colonial interests. It had even signed treaties with Japan specifically to help combat Russian expansionism.

Britain went to war in support of Belgium. It had guaranteed Belgium neutrality under the Treaty of London (1839) and intended to honour it. The Germans had greatly underestimated Britain's commitment to the treaty, disregarding it as just 'a scrap of paper' although they too were signatories. Many among the German high command thought that Britain would renege once the Schlieffen Plan was in full swing and remain neutral. What did it hope to gain? Britain had no territorial ambitions in continental Europe. What they failed to understand was that Britain simply couldn't let large swathes of Europe fall into German hands. Britain could not abide – or indeed survive – the formation of a huge German Empire just off its coast. It had to fight.

Original Kitchener World War I Recruitment poster **1914.**

BRITONS

"WANTS YOU"

JOIN YOUR COUNTRY'S ARMY!
GOD SAVE THE KING

Reproduced by permission of LONDON OPINION

Gunners setting fuses for a British QF 13 pounder Mk IV anti-aircraft gun, 4th Division, British Expeditionary Force, **Nieppe, France.**

"A" Company of the 4th Battalion, Royal Fusiliers (9th Brigade, 3rd Division) resting in the square at Mons, Belgium. **22 August, 1914.**

"The trumpet calls", an Australian Army recruitment poster from World War I.

Major-General Sir Henry Timson Lukin.

British soldiers kit.

The British set Germany an ultimatum – to respect Belgian neutrality or else. On 3rd August, at 11pm, that ultimatum expired. The very next day, a Bank Holiday Monday, Great Britain declared war on Imperial Germany. The Foreign Office released a statement to the world:

'Owing to the summary rejection by the German Government of the request made by His Majesty's Government for assurances that the neutrality of Belgium would be respected, His Majesty's Ambassador in Berlin has received his passport, and His Majesty's Government has declared to the German Government that a state of war exists between Great Britain and Germany as from 11pm on August 4th.'

An instruction was sent out to the armed forces. It comprised just three words:

'WAR. GERMANY. ACT'.

As the British Expeditionary Force prepared to ship out to France, the Royal Navy moved into the North Sea in force to start blockading Germany and denying her supplies.

THE BRITISH EXPEDITIONARY FORCE IN 1914

'It is my Royal and Imperial command that you concentrate your energies, for the immediate present, upon one single purpose, and that is that you address all your skill and all the valour of my soldiers to exterminate first the treacherous English and walk over General French's contemptible little army.'

Alleged order issued to the German Imperial Armies by Kaiser Wilhelm II, 19th August 1914

In the actuality of war on the continent, it had been planned to send six divisions of the regular British Army and a further division of cavalry to join the war effort. In the event, two divisions were initially held back when the British Expeditionary Force embarked for Europe, for fear of a German invasion attempt on mainland Britain. Those two Divisions were released and despatched to fight in Europe in late August and September 1914, when responsibility for home defence was switched to territorial forces.

The BEF was under the overall command of Field Marshal Sir John Denton Pinkstone French, a man who had started his military career in the Royal Navy but who had swiftly switched to the cavalry after discovering that he suffered from violent and crippling seasickness.

There was no doubt that the BEF comprised some of the finest soldiers in the world. However these were men primarily trained to fight colonial wars rather than a grand continental war and their numbers were miniscule when compared with both French and German regular troops deployed in the field. By September, the BEF only numbered around 120,000 men. By the end of 1914, the vast majority of these men would be dead or wounded.

In total, Britain's army in 1914 comprised some 700,000 men, including those of the Territorial Force Reserve. France, by comparison had over 4 million men under arms and Germany almost six million.

SOLDIERS OF THE DOMINION

As an Imperial world power, Britain could call on the help of military forces from countries throughout the Empire – and very quickly did so.

The Indian Expeditionary Force arrived on the field of battle within two months of war breaking out. They fought in the Battle of La Bassée in October 1914 and led the offensive in the Battle of Neuve Chapelle in March 1915. However, the Indian soldiers found adapting to the climate of continental Europe extremely difficult and the IEF's fighting capabilities were further hampered by both unfamiliarity with weapons like the Lee Enfield rifle and with difficulties in replacing dead British officers who could command. The Indian Corps were eventually reassigned away from the Western Front to Egypt.

The South Africans, under Brigadier General Henry

German troops in Blankenberge, Belgium, World War I.

The execution of Belgian notables **1914**.

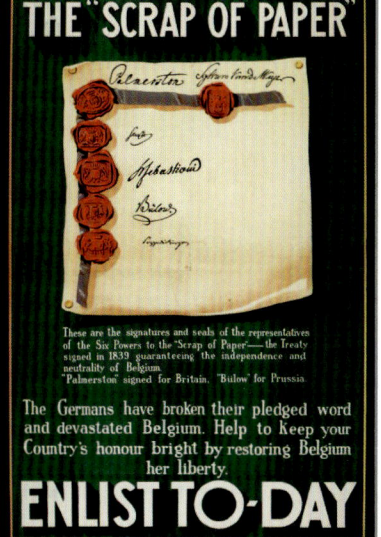

This British poster encouraged enlistment by arousing sympathy for Belgium.

Lukin, provided four infantry battalions and five Heavy Artillery batteries. Fighting on the Somme and at Passchendaele, the South Africans were to suffer one of the grimmest attrition rates of the war with some 5,000 men killed and another 15,000 wounded.

The Australian Imperial Force (AIF) would grow from an initial 20,000 men to five full infantry divisions over the course of the war. All were volunteers. They were first deployed on the Western Front in June 1916, under British command and considered part of British forces for two years. Battle honours would include the Somme, Ypres, Bullecourt and Passchendaele.

The Canadian Expeditionary Force, initially commanded by General Edwin Anderson, grew to some four infantry divisions over the course of the war. Over half a million men served. The Canadians always served as part of a British Army but distinguished themselves in their own right. Battle honours included the Second Battle of Ypres, the Somme, Vimy Ridge and Passchendaele. They would also help to spearhead the 100 Days Offensive in 1918.

The soldiers of the New Zealand Expeditionary Force (along with the Australians) were rated by Britain and Germany alike as some of the toughest and most resilient men on the field of battle and consequently were often used as 'shock troops' by the Allies. Initially deployed to the disastrous Gallipoli Campaign in the Dardanelles, they would serve on the Western Front from April 1916 onwards.

THE RAPE OF BELGIUM

'We will teach them to respect Germany!'
unknown German officer, during the burning of the Louvain University Library

The Germans swept into Luxembourg on 2nd August, the buckles on their army belts bearing the inscription *Got mit uns* (God is with us). Luxembourg had no army of its own and was helpless to resist. The same day the German government wrote to their Belgian counterparts requesting unopposed passage for their armies through

Belgium so that they could attack France. The Belgians refused. The Germans were unperturbed. They held the small and old fashioned Belgian Army in utter contempt.

On 3rd August they moved into Belgium. Leaflets were widely distributed by the Germans apologising for the invasion but claiming they had had to act because of French forces already invading Belgium - in disguise. It went on to promise that Belgians should consider the German soldiers as 'the best of friends' and expressed the hope that the invaders would not have to fight the Belgians. But fight the Belgians did.

A day later advanced German forces attacked Liege, a beautiful medieval city defended by twelve heavily defended forts. The Germans had allowed 2 days to take Liege. In reality, its forts held out for 12 days, severely disrupting the German timetable. Only the use of massive Krupp and Skoda artillery pieces succeeded in cracking the forts, pieces like the legendary 'Big Bertha' (named after the industrialist Gustav Krupps' somewhat corpulent wife).

Now the full might of the German 1st, 2nd and 3rd Armies descended on the nation, sweeping ever south and east towards the French borders at a speed sometimes of 30 miles a day. Brussels fell on 20th August.

The Germans were stunned by the resistance they encountered. They were simply outraged by the audacity of the Belgians in actually fighting them. At the same time they were utterly paranoid about the prospect of Belgian guerrilla fighters, having had serious problems with the French during the Franco-Prussian War. There were none, but as lines of communication failed and discipline broke down', German units began to attack each other in chaotic 'friendly fire' incidents – and then were quick to blame Belgian resistance fighters rather than themselves.

The Germans instigated a policy of 'collective responsibility' which meant that, if they met with any resistance, they would round up local civilians – men, women and children – and summarily execute them. 156 were killed at Aarschot, where there were also widespread incidents of rape. 211 civilians were shot at Andenne and 383 at Tamines. At the site of the worst atrocities, Dinant, a total of 674 civilians were murdered by the command of General August von Hausen. The oldest was in his nineties, the youngest just a month old. Some were shot, others bayoneted or burned alive. In total 60,000 Belgian civilians died, 6,000 of who were executed by their occupiers. One British writer described the German Army in Belgium as *one vast gang of Jack the Rippers'*.

Political cartoon from **Punch** showing a Belgian farmer standing up to the German aggressor. **12 August 1914.**

BRAVO, BELGIUM!

Concrete-emplaced predecessor to the **Big Bertha** German 420-mm howitzer of World War I.

German machine gunners in action with a **MG08.**

General Paul Pau, head of the **"Army of Alsace".**

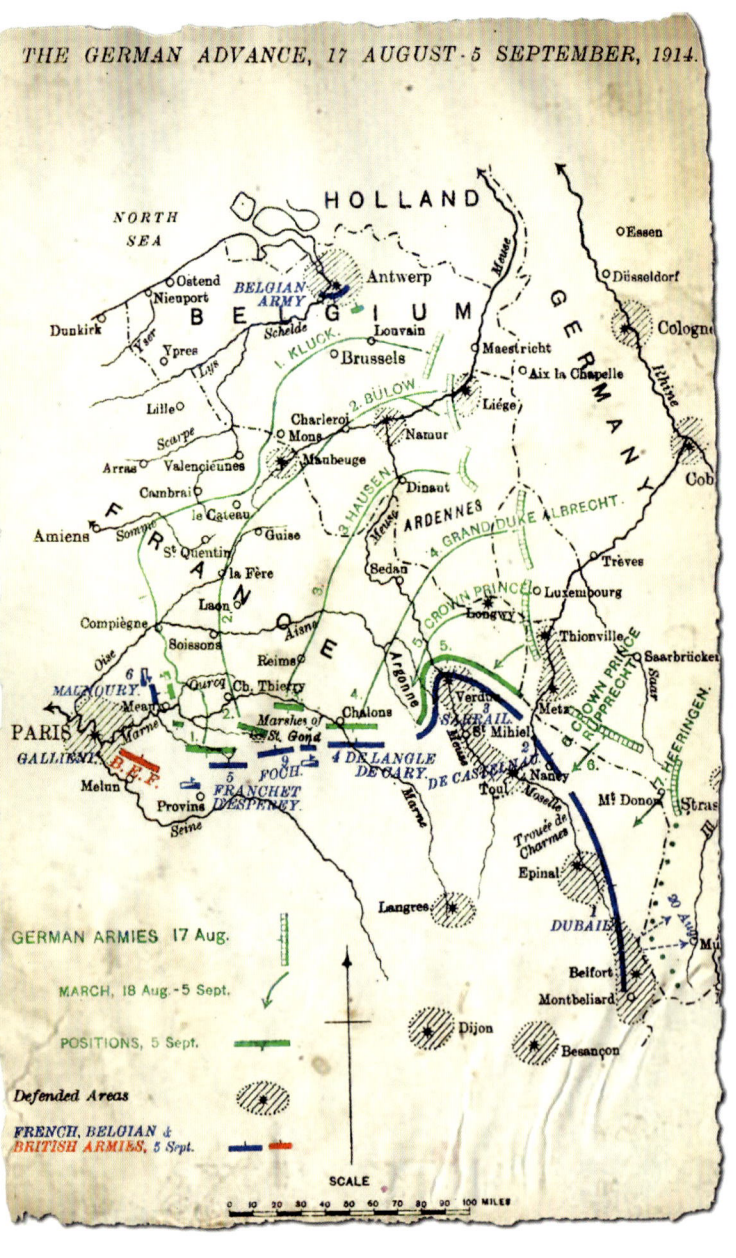

THE GERMAN ADVANCE, 17 AUGUST - 5 SEPTEMBER, 1914.

Map showing German advance in France, from 17th August - 5th September 1914.

As the Germans pressed on, a full twenty per cent of the population of Belgium became refugees, fleeing out of the cities, towns and villages ahead of the invading army. King Albert I of Belgium and his government retreated to the port city of Antwerp, which managed to resist until the 8th October, by which time the King and his government had escaped to Le Havre along with a good portion of the army.

Reports of the German atrocities soon reached the press in Britain and outraged the public. Many were true. The Germans were on occasion acting like beasts, raping and murdering en masse. However, there was an element of some stories growing in the telling, as British politicians saw the propaganda value, both on the Home Front and abroad, especially in America. Now, Allied soldiers were reported to have been crucified and then burned alive. Babies were torn from their mothers' breasts, thrown to the ground and bayoneted. Other babies were eaten. In the main, however, propaganda focused on the abuse of women, with numerous stories being circulated of rapes and sexual mutilations being committed by the German invaders. In one particularly bizarre story, nuns were said to have been stripped and strapped to church bells. They were then dashed to death against one another as German soldiers stood below, pulling furiously on the bell ropes. The reality of the German atrocities committed in Belgium was much more mundane but no less sickening.

THE BATTLE OF THE FRONTIERS

The French too had their pre-war battle plans. As the Germans swept into Belgium, the French put Plan XVII into action. Part of Plan XVII was a concerted effort to retake the provinces of Alsace and Lorraine, which had been lost to the Germans in the Franco-Prussian War. They would then press on to the Rhine and total victory in their glorious, brightly coloured red and blue battledress. The German defences, it had been decided by the military planners, would crack wide open because of the sheer 'flair and guts' of the fighting Frenchman. The bayonet would be the weapon of choice. French armies would be trained only in the art of attack and never in that of defence. That was la gloire. It all looked good on paper.

On 7th August, the French Commander-in-Chief General Joseph Joffre, known to his men as 'Papa', put the plan into motion and the French VII Corps struck against Alsace. On 8th August, there was great national celebration in France when VII Corps liberated the undefended town of Mulhouse. When they lost it to a German counterattack the very next day, the nation was shaken. On 14th August the French launched a larger offensive against Lorraine with the might of its 1st and 2nd Armies. Here they met the German 6th and 7th under Crown Prince Rupprecht of Bavaria and quickly sustained grievous losses assaulting well-fortified German positions. Lieutenant Edward Spears, then a British Liaison Officer with the French, wrote:

'The gallant officers who led them were entirely ignorant of the stopping power of modern firearms, and many of them thought it chic to die in white gloves'.

Although ordered to fight a holding, defensive battle, Rupprecht instead went on the offensive. Both French armies were thrown back, and the VII Corps in Alsace were forced to retreat to survive as well. By 22nd August the French were effectively back where they had started. Behind them, flush with victory, German units went on the rampage. 50 civilians in the French border town of Nomeny were shot or bayoneted to death, while the town itself was looted and burned.

As communications broke down, Joffre struggled desperately to keep up with events happening all over the battlefield – a foretaste of problems that all commanders would soon face. He requisitioned a French triple-winning grand prix racing driver and had him chauffeur the Commander all over the battlefield to find out what was going on.

Even as the war in Lorraine waged, French forces in the Ardennes suddenly found themselves facing a build-up of German forces. Plan XVII hadn't anticipated this. The two sides met in dense fog in the middle of thick forest on 21st August – and not surprisingly there was total confusion on both sides, with nobody having any good idea where the enemy was or in what strength. Things went particularly badly for the French though. They were wearing bright coloured uniforms that were easier to see in the fog; the Germans had good defences prepared, including camouflaged machine gun nests – and there were a lot more Germans than anyone realised. Two days later, the French were in full retreat, streaming back hotly pursued by the German 5th.

General Sir Horace Smith-Dorrien.

French General Charles Lanrezac.

Alexander von Kluck.

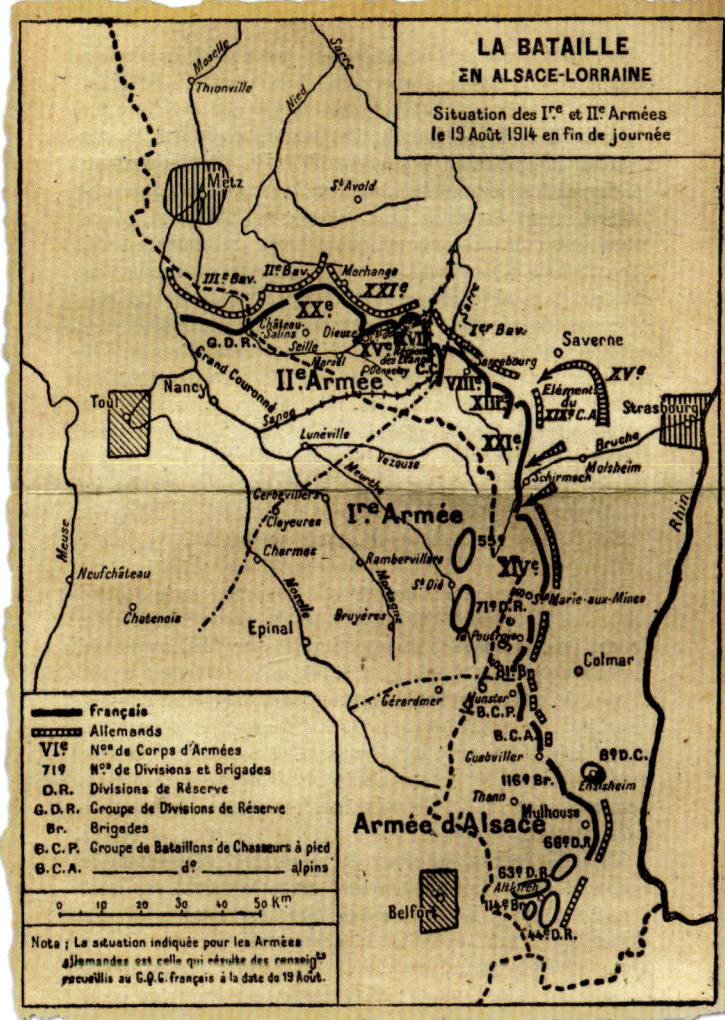

The same day as the French and Germans clashed in the Ardennes, the French 5th Army on the Belgian Frontier found itself straight in the path of the advancing German 2nd Army as it streamed across the Sambre River. By 23rd August, the French 5th was in full retreat, streaming back towards Paris.

On 24th August, the French President Raymond Poincare wrote in his diary, ' *Now the future of France depends on her powers of resistance.'*

MONS

By 14th August 1914, the British Expeditionary Force comprising some 90,000 men had arrived on the coast of Europe and almost immediately received orders to link up with General Lanrezac's 5th French Army defending the Belgian border. They marched confidently through the continental country lanes singing an abusive song about German royalty and the commander of the German Ist Army, General Alexander Heinrich Rudolph von Kluck :

'Kaiser Bill is feeling ill
The Crown Prince has gone barmy.
We don't give a f*** for old von Kluck
And all his bleedin' army'

The men of the BEF were seasoned professional soldiers. Their main armament was the .303 Lee Enfield rifle, augmented by a 17 inch long steel bayonet. Each man was fully capable of aiming and firing at 15 different targets per minute at a range of 300 yards – a lethal rate. They were well supported by machine gunners. cavalry units, a range of artillery units and a new novelty – reconnaissance aircraft.

On 21st August, the BEF began to get into skirmishes with German cavalry troops. This told French that more heavyweight German units were nearby and he started to make plans to attack. Fortunately he didn't carry them through – as the number of German troops heading his way was far greater than he could possibly have imagined, some 90,000 men from the German Ist under Kluck. The BEF had just 30,000 men in the immediate area.

The British arrived in Mons on 22nd August. It was a grubby, drab, run down mining town with an industrial canal running through it. To their right, the French 5th

Army was already locked in fierce combat with the Germans. The French commander, General Lanrezac, implored the BEF to deploy itself along the southern banks of the Belgian Mons-Conde Canal to protect his left flank from the oncoming German 1st Army, which could otherwise smash into his already beleaguered and hard-pressed forces from the side.

The BEF split in two, with II Corps taking up positions along the canal as requested, under the command of Sir Horace Smith-Dorrien. I Corps under Sir Douglas Haig took up positions to defend I Corp's right flank in case the French 5th Army suddenly collapsed.

The German attack on II Corps began at dawn on Sunday, 23rd August with a ferocious artillery barrage to the sound of church bells. At 9am, a massed German infantry assault commenced, aiming to seize four vital bridges over the canal. The British soldiers were stunned to see their enemies marching in tight columns to the bridges as if they were still on the parade ground. The Germans were torn to pieces in short order by a combination of British machine guns, supporting artillery and rapid, dense rifle fire. The rifle fire in particular was so intense that German officers feared they were facing an army with 28 machine guns in every battalion. In reality, each battalion had only two.

The Germans quickly learned their lesson. When they came again, it was in loose waves. Now the machine guns stationed at the British ends of the bridges would prove critical in making the Germans pay a heavy price. However, the sheer weight of the German assault proved to be unstoppable and, by the afternoon of the 23rd, the British had had to abandon their canal side positions and fall back to new defensive lines slightly further south.

In the early hours of 24th August, Sir John French received the news he had been dreading. The French 5th was falling back in hard and heavy retreat. The Allied line had collapsed. French wanted to take his forces back to the coast but Kitchener, the British Secretary of State for War, overruled him. The BEF was to join the general retreat and fall back south east with the French Armies. The BEF would fight a number of desperate and ferocious rear-guard actions as it fell back, protecting the rear of the main bulk of its troops. The retreat would not stop for 13 days and 150 miles.

Despite the BEF having to retreat from Mons, they had achieved much. They had prevented the annihilation of the French 5th by successfully defending its flank.

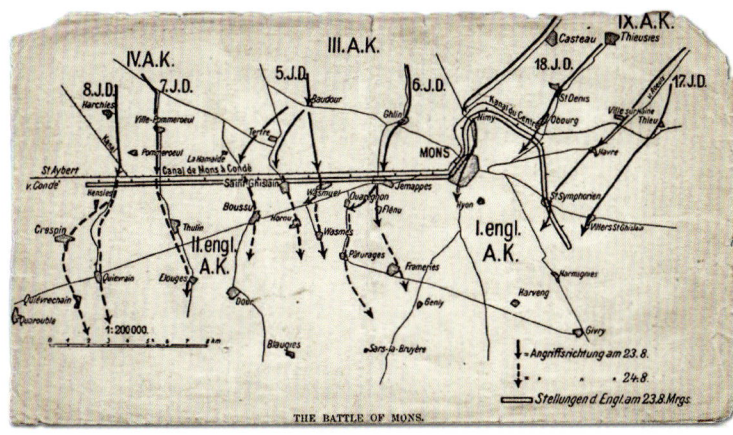

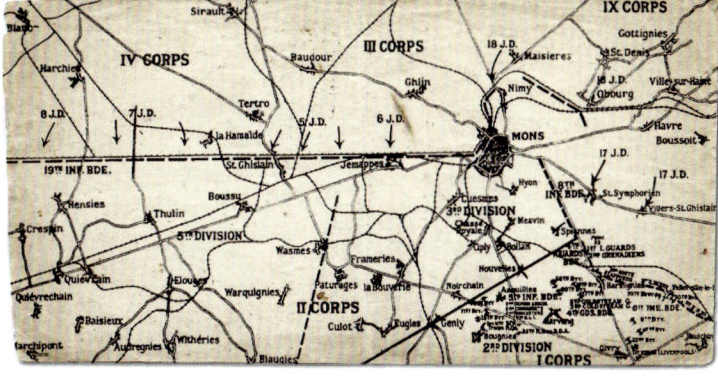

Portrait of **Field Marshal Earl Kitchener** of **Khartoum**, in full dress uniform and carrying his Field Marshal's Baton.

German soldiers on the front at the
First Battle of the Marne.

French soldiers lying in personal trenches.

They had also delayed the Germans in the execution of their time-sensitive Schlieffen Plan by one or two critical days. They had proven themselves a small but formidable fighting force and inflicted heavy losses on the enemy. BEF casualties were 1,600 men. German losses were estimated to be in excess of 5,000.

One German infantry officer at Mons later recalled how badly his men had been mauled by the BEF:

'The men all chilled to the bone, almost too exhausted to move and with the depressing consciousness of defeat weighing heavily upon them. A bad defeat, there can be no gainsaying it... we had been badly beaten, and by the English – by the English we had so laughed at a few hours before.'

The German losses were so severe – and so shocking – that von Kluck paused to reconsider his position rather than setting off in immediate pursuit of the retreating BEF. After the war, he would praise the BEF as 'an incomparable army'.

THE FIRST TO DIE

The first British soldier to die in action on the Western Front during World War one was 16-year-old Private John Parr of the 4th Battalion, the Middlesex Regiment. A former golf caddy from North Finchley, Parr had joined the army to better himself and see the world and had lied about his age to join up.

On 21st August 1914, along with a fellow soldier, Parr had bicycled into the small Belgian village of Obourg, just to the north-east of Mons, on a reconnaissance mission. The two soldiers encountered a German cavalry patrol from the 1st Army and Parr elected to provide covering fire as his fellow soldier cycled back to report. He was shot dead.

His grave is in the St. Symphorien Military Cemetery, directlyfacing the grave of the last British soldier to die in the war.

A British civilian, a teacher named Henry Hadley, had already been murdered by German soldiers on 3rd August 1914. He was travelling on a train in Germany when he got into an altercation with several military officers which ended with him making rude gestures at them. One then pursued him from the train's dining car and shot him dead in his seat, claiming that he thought he might be a spy.

'KITCHENER'S MOB'

'The Women of Britain Say Go!
Recruitment poster slogan

It's often said that the British were under the delusion that this would be a short war and it would, to quote the famous phrase, 'all be over by Christmas'. This is not true. Virtually everyone in Britain from politicians to generals, soldiers to civilians knew this could well be a protracted and hard-fought fight. It was the Kaiser who had promised his troops embarking for Belgium and France that they would be back 'before the leaves fell'.

When the BEF was despatched for France, it comprised around half of the regular British Army. The rest was scattered around colonial outposts throughout the world and would take time to bring home, reequip and despatch to the continent. Britain could also call upon its territorial forces and reservists as well as Dominion forces – but all together this would not add up to an army the size of those being deployed by the French and Germans. Britain was primarily a naval power. Its strength lay in its dreadnoughts, not its army.

Something needed to be done – and fast.

Lord Horatio Herbert Kitchener, then the British Secretary of State for War, anticipated that the conflict could last for as long as three years and boil down to the last million fighting men. He rapidly set about raising a 'New Army' of volunteers with his face staring out of posters that bore the blunt statement ' Your country needs you'.

The bestial German behaviour in Belgium, combined with a wave of sheer patriotism, resulted in a huge tide of volunteers from the outset. Recruitment offices were regularly overwhelmed by queues of volunteers over a mile long. There were nowhere near enough uniforms or rifles to keep up. Men were signed up at mass rallies, at their workplaces and at football games. The stars of music hall did their bit too. Marie Lloyd held recruiting drives at her shows, singing:

'I didn't like yer much before yer join'd the army, John. But I do like yer, cocky, now you've got yer Khaki on.'

Poster, produced by E V Kealey in 1915 for the British army recruitment campaign.

French infantrymen bayonet charge.

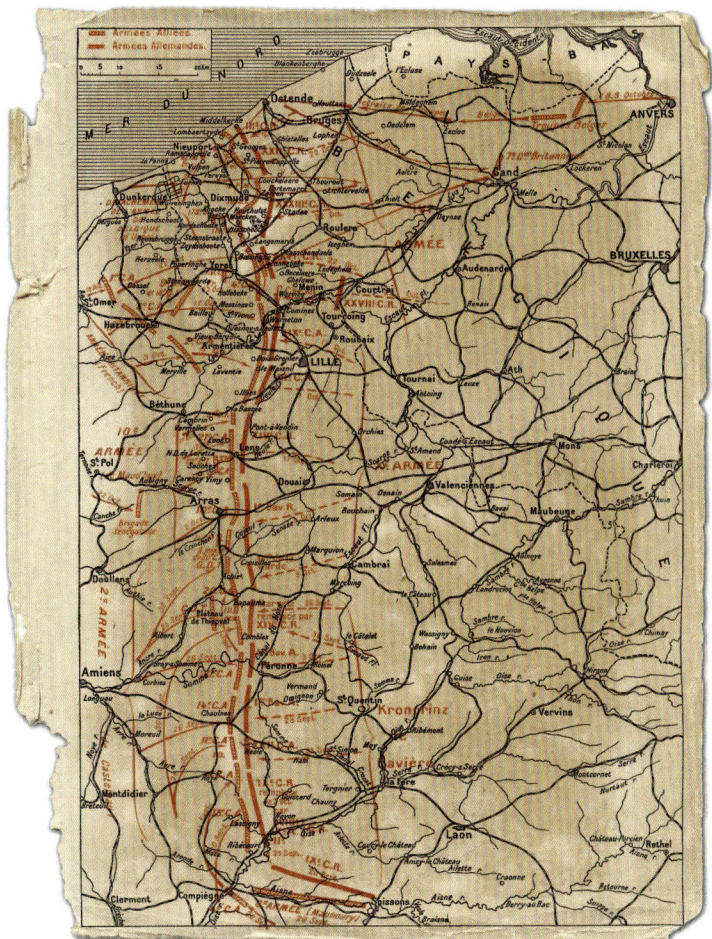
French map of the "race to the sea" during World War 1 1914.

Harry Lauder, lacking the same saucy sex appeal, resorted to offering a tenner to the first man to join him on stage and sign up. His own son would be killed in the war.

One recruiting innovation – later to backfire with tragic and devastating consequences – was the idea Pals Battalions, thought up by BEF General Sir Henry Rawlinson. Friends from one town or city could all sign up and serve together in the same unit. There were also to be Pals Battalions based on professions, like the Artists' Battalion and the Sportsmans' Battalion. There were even Public Schoolboys Battalions and 'Bantam Battalions' for men who couldn't quite muster the 5' 3 required to serve in the regular army. There was fierce competition between towns to raise the most Pals Battalions.

Kitchener hoped for 500,000 volunteers. He got two and a half million, each man volunteering for three years (or the duration of the war). The first elements of Kitchener's New Army saw service at the Battle of Loos in 1915. The main force of arrived just in time for the Somme. For many bright enthusiastic volunteers, their first experience of combat would be to go over the top and walk slowly towards the enemy on the fateful first day.

They were, in those terrible words of Private A.V. Pearson of the Leeds Pals:

'...two years in the making and ten minutes in the destroying.'

THE FIRST BATTLE OF THE MARNE

German forces pursuing the retreating French and the BEF were now just 30 miles from Paris. The capital made desperate attempts to fortify, while half a million Parisians became refugees and the French government fled the city for the relative safety of Bordeaux. Demolition charges were strapped to the Eiffel Tower, in case it fell to the enemy, while the American military attaché reported 'mutterings against the leaders of the government and army'. It looked to be all over. As G.K. Chesterton wrote, 'the world waited for the doom of the city.'

Now, however the German commanders made a serious tactical error, thanks in part to the arch rivalry between Generals von Kluck and von Bulow, commanders of the 1st and 2nd Armies. The Armies had both received a mauling at the hands of the Allies and were now both more badly stretched and more poorly supplied than had been anticipated by this stage of the campaign. Furthermore the Russians had mobilised quicker than anticipated and large numbers of soldiers were taken from Moltke's western armies to shore up the eastern defences. Kluck decided to pass east of Paris instead of west, as the Schlieffen Plan originally intended. As the German 1st and 2nd bunched up, they exposed their flank to the Allies.

Joffre spotted their mistake and, on 6th September, ordered his secretly assembled new 6th Army into action. The German 1st wheeled to meet them and stunted their attack, but in doing so opened up a 30 mile gap between the German 1st and 2nd. After the gap was spotted by reconnaissance aeroplanes, Allied forces from the French 5th and the BEF poured in to attack. The Germans thought they could fight their way out through the 6th, but it was quickly reinforced and reinvigorated by the arrival of 10,000 French reserves, 6,000 of whom were transported to the front from Paris in commandeered taxi cabs.

Communications between Berlin and the front line started to fail. Moltke gave orders for his men to 'Stand fast' but his idea of their position was out of date and they had to retreat for two days to get to the required position. The troops – and their generals – were thoroughly demoralised. The instructions they were getting simply didn't make sense on the battlefield anymore. Realizing he was losing his grip on the situation, Moltke could be found sitting at his map table, crying into cupped hands. By 9th September, the German position looked increasing hopeless. With the gap widening between the German 1st and 2nd, communications broke down further and co-ordinated action was impossible. Unless something drastic was done, both the 1st and 2nd Armies faced the prospect of encirclement and then annihilation. Chief of the German General Staff Moltke – the man who had once said, 'War! And the sooner the better!' - responded to the threat by having a co mplete nervous breakdown, raving about the horrors of war to his wife and anyone else who would listen. His subordinates in the field took charge and hastily organised a retreat to positions north of the Marne River and close by the Aisne River where they dug in furiously.

The German dream of a lightning victory was over.

Hell fight on the Aisne river. Poster shows a side view of a German soldier in battle.

French map showing the positions of the **Belgian, French, British** and **German** armies on **1st September 1914**, the beginning of the **Battle of the Marr**

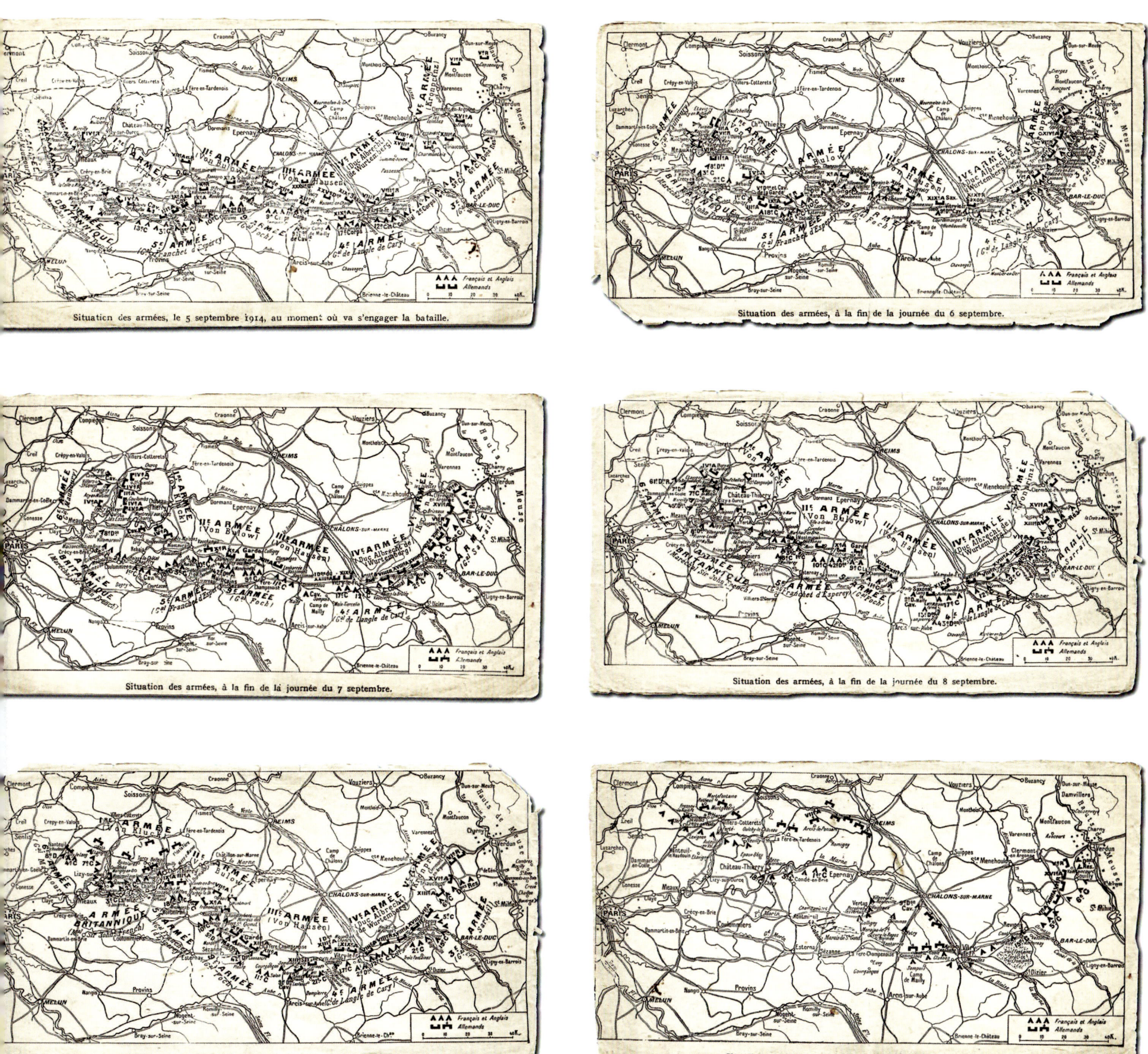

Situation des armées, le 5 septembre 1914, au moment où va s'engager la bataille.

Situation des armées, à la fin de la journée du 6 septembre.

Situation des armées, à la fin de la journée du 7 septembre.

Situation des armées, à la fin de la journée du 8 septembre.

Situation des armées, à la fin de la journée du 9 septembre.

Situation générale, à la fin de la journée du 10 septembre.

French maps showing day by day battle progress from 6th - 10th September 1914 **first battle of the Marne.**

Painting of the **2nd Oxfordshire** and **Buckinghamshire Light Infantry** fighting the **Prussian Guard** at the **Battle of Nonne Bosschen.**

129th (Duke of Connaught's Own) Baluchis (now **11 Baloch, Pakistan Army**) near **Hollebeke, Belgium, First Battle of Ypres.**

The Schlieffen Plan had failed and the mass assault had been fought to a standstill. There was no plan for this eventuality. The best Germany could do now was to dig in and hold. It had suffered 220,000 casualties in the battle. A partially recovered von Moltke told his Kaiser, 'Your Majesty, we have lost the war'. He was unceremoniously replaced by Erich von Falkenhayn as Chief of the General Staff.

THE 'RACE TO THE SEA'

When the Battle of the Marne ground to a terrible stalemate with opposing trench lines, it was everything that commanders and tacticians on both sides had feared.

Everyone understood that stalemate would lead to trench warfare – and everyone understood what trench warfare would mean. Defending forces would enjoy a huge advantage thanks to machine guns and barbed wire, further reinforcing stalemate. Nothing could move without being impaled on wire or shot to death in the terrible spaces between the lines. Artillery might make a difference, but only if the battlefield were allowed to become one vast meat grinder – and well-prepared trenches could survive bombardment.

Just a couple of months after the outbreak of hostilities, the commanders had a very good idea what this war was going to look like – so they made one last, desperate attempt to break the stalemate. The conventional way of defeating a heavily fortified enemy position was not to assault it headlong but to outflank it, making the breakthrough at a less fortified place in the lines and then assaulting the fortification from the more vulnerable sides or rear.

So began the 'Race to the Sea', with the Germans fighting ever westward, trying to get around the right flank of the ever-growing Allied defensive lines before they could be completed. The Allies tried the same, striking away at the German's left flank as they too extended their trench networks westward. Nothing worked. One Army would try a flanking manoeuvre, only to run straight into the enemy trying to execute their own flanking manoeuvre on the same ground. Both would then dig in and hold. There was no great breakthrough and - by October 1914 - there was just one last place left where the opposing Armies might break through... Ypres in Belgium.

THE FIRST BATTLE OF YPRES

The First Battle of Ypres in Belgium was the culmination of the 'Race to the Sea'. It was Germany's last chance to outflank the Allies, break through to the Channel Ports of Calais, Dunkirk and Boulogne and disrupt the BEF's supply lines. The war could still be won in 1914. The Allies also saw an opportunity to recapture Belgium and then to press on to Germany from the south and west.

The Germans committed their 4th and 6th Armies against a defensive line of French, Belgian and British troops. They struck first on October 20th. Actions against the Belgians led to King Albert ordering sea sluice gates to be opened. 27 miles of low lying land was flooded with tumultuous sea water, halting the Germans and forcing them to reconsider their plans.

Now Falkenhayn threw himself at the town of Ypres and the numerically smaller British forces defending it. After initial success, they were driven back by a determined British counterattack – and once again British rifle fire was so fierce that it was mistaken by the Germans for machine gun fire. On 11th November, the Germans broke through at Nun's Wood, just 4 miles from the city, but were repulsed by a rag-tag force of British cooks, medical orderlies, clerks and officers' batmen hastily assembled to save the day.

Attacks and counter-attacks on both sides continued until the 22nd November but petered out due to increasingly awful weather conditions combining heavy rain with driving snow. The Germans had been held – but at a high cost to the BEF. It had proved to be the largest battle the BEF had fought since the start of the war and British casualties were said to be 51,155 killed, wounded or missing – all experienced professional soldiers which the British Army could scarcely afford to lose. French losses were given as 50,000. German casualties were put at 155,000. Ypres had seen the baptism of fire for many fresh German troops raced to the front line. They had been given just six weeks training and many faced the guns with arms linked together, singing traditional student drinking songs. The Germans referred to this, mournfully, as Der Kindermord von Ypern – the massacre of the innocents at Ypres.

Erich von Falkenhayn, Chief of the General Staff of the German Army.

German Trenches on the Aisne.

Trench Raid charcoal on board
by Harold James Mowat .

World War I Daily Mail Official War Photograph, Series IX, No. 70,
titled "British infantry practising an attack".

THE TRENCHES

'It was 9 a.m. and the so-called trench was full of corpses and all sorts of equipment. We stood and sat on bodies as if they were stones or logs of wood. Nobody worried if one had its head stuck through or torn off, or a third had gory bones sticking out through its torn coat. And outside the trench one could see them lying in every kind of position.'
a BEF soldier, 1914.

The first trenches on the Western Front were dug out of immediate need on the battlefield. Then, as the 'Race to the Sea' blazed west and north, those hastily constructed temporary defences began to join up and become something more permanent. By December 1914, each side had its own trench lines, stretching some 475 miles from the North Sea at Dixmuide to Belfort on the Swiss Border. Eleven million French and Belgian citizens remained trapped helplessly behind the German lines, subject to cruel discipline and deprivation. The Germans had also captured most of France's coal mines and heavy industry.

The trench lines varied according to where they were and how strong the opposing forces were in that area. In places they were formidable, elaborate and major constructs. In others they might amount to little more than crude earthworks and defensive mounds of earth. The trench lines were not straight: They deliberately zig-zagged every so often to prevent any enemy soldiers who succeeded in infiltrating the line from being able to shoot any distance down the trench. The trenches also typically comprised three separates trench lines. The first line – or 'Front Line' was exposed to the enemy, and usually relatively lightly manned unless an attack was expected, as it was most vulnerable to artillery and snipers, Behind that would be a second 'support' trench in which troops could shelter and still further back a third 'assembly' trench where attacking forces could muster and wait before going

forward. These three lines could be anything from 300 to 1200 feet apart, and were intersected by communications trenches allowing access to different levels of the defence. Advanced observation and raiding positions known as saps might also be dug outwards into No Man's Land. In many places there would also be a completely separate trench line system, perhaps a couple of miles behind the first, into which troops could retreat if they were attacked with overwhelming force.

Certainly, in the early years of the war, the construction of the German trenches was superior to the Allies, with more use made of concrete blockhouses and shelters that could descend some four storeys below ground. The Germans were here to hold their positions and their captured ground. The Allies needed to move forward and liberate that ground, driving the Germans back to their borders. They expected to shift position and built with less of a sense of permanence.

Typically, the distance between opposing trench lines – the space known as No Man's Land – was somewhere between 300 and 900 feet although in places, such as Vimy Ridge, the lines could close to as little as 90 feet apart.

The first – 'fighting' – line of trenches were usually around 12 foot deep, but could be much shallower. BEF units gave them names, typically the names of fighting units or sometimes, more ironically, names like 'Park Lane' or 'Mayfair'. In a typical year, a British soldier could expect his unit to spend around 15% of the time at the sharpest end of the trench system and in the greatest danger. He would be a front line soldier for a week at a time. 40% of the time he would play a supporting or reserve function. 'Rest' constituted approximately 1/5th of the soldier's year.

By day, looking over the parapet or moving about in No Man's Land was tantamount to suicide. Most activity happened at night. Raiding parties might be sent over to take prisoners and glean intelligence, or else the night might be devoted to repairing holes in the wire or moving supplies.

Typhoid, Cholera, Trench Fever and Dysentery soon became commonplace, fed by overflowing latrines or the rotting, unburied dead – some of whom became embedded in the trench walls during long offensives. Almost everyone was infested with

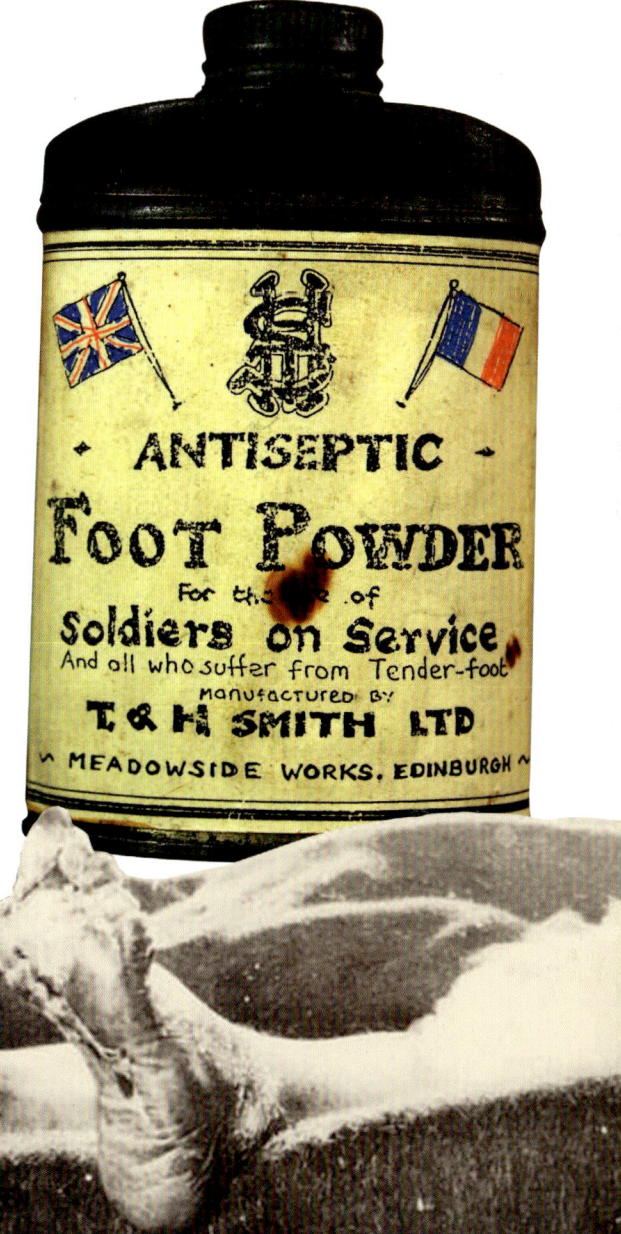

Case of trench feet suffered by unidentified soldier .
ABOVE: Antiseptic foot powder produced by **T & H Smith LTD** .

German soldiers of the **134th Saxon Regiment** photographed with men of the **Royal Warwickshire Regiment** in No Man's Land.

British and German troops meeting in No-Man's Land during the unofficial truce. British troops are from the **Northumberland Hussars, 7th Division, Bridoux-Rouge Banc Sector.**

German Christmas card from 1914 reading "Merry Christmas and Happy New Year".

head and body lice, while fungal infections like Trench Mouth or Trench Foot proved a daily torture. Untreated, they could turn gangrenous and require amputation. The stink, from overfilled latrines, from decomposing corpses, from gunpowder and unwashed men was chronic. So too was the overpowering smell of Creosol and chloride of lime, spread everywhere to try and limit the spread of disease.

In winter, more men fell victim to exposure. Rain for much of the year could fill the bottoms of trenches with vile liquid mud, mixed with effluent from the latrines which overwhelmed the wooden duckboards of the trench floor and came lapping over the boot-tops of the soldiers. Trench walls would need shoring up regularly to stop the soggy filth from collapsing in on the occupants.

Rats ran rampant. Gorging themselves stupid on the choice liver and eyes of the unburied dead (and the helpless wounded), they would grow unnaturally to the size of cats and swarmed in their millions. They only seemed to disappear shortly before an enemy artillery attack. Many soldiers swore blind that the rats had some kind of 'sixth sense' about impending danger. Some tried to make pets of them. Others spent idle hours trying to shoot or club as many as they could until they gave up with the sheer weight of numbers.

In short, life was a mixture of long periods of boredom and misery, punctuated by moments of stark terror and confusion.

THE CHRISTMAS TRUCE

As the Allies and the German forces settled into their trenches, there was stalemate – and a strange thing started to happen. Ad hoc, small scale ceasefires and truces began to occur. Opposing sides agreed to stop shooting so that the dead and wounded could be retrieved from the battlefield. Soldiers from opposing sides would pop out of their trenches to chat with each other, or to swap rations for cigarettes. Agreements were made whereby no-one would shoot while the soldiers were taking a break or a spot of exercise. The fraternization became so relaxed in some places that French senior officers started to fear that their men would no longer see the Germans as their enemies. General Sir Horace Smith-Dorrien shared a view held by many fellow British officers when he said he saw

a danger of his men quickly developing a 'live-and-let-live' attitude to the enemy. 'Friendly intercourse with the enemy', he said, should be 'absolutely prohibited.'

One soldier from the Royal Engineers described a breakfast truce in a letter home:

'Perhaps it will surprise you to learn that the soldiers in both lines of trenches have become very 'pally' with each other. The trenches are only 60 yards apart at one place, and every morning about breakfast time one of the soldiers sticks a board in the air. As soon as this board goes up all firing ceases, and men from either side draw their water and rations. All through the breakfast hour, and so long as this board is up, silence reigns supreme, but whenever the board comes down the first unlucky devil who shows even so much as a hand gets a bullet through it.'

Things came to a head over the Christmas of 1914. Around Ypres on Christmas Eve, the Germans adorned their trenches with Christmas trees and paper decorations, lit candles and then started singing carols. The British joined in with Christmas favourites from their lines. A German marching band began to play God Save the King. There were shouts of *'Merry Christmas!'* and then men climbed out of their respective trenches into No Man's Land where they exchanged handshakes, souvenirs and gifts. One British machine gunner was even reported to have given a German soldier a haircut with his wire cutters. On Christmas Day – when there was snow on the ground in some places - a number of impromptu soccer matches were indeed held, sometimes featuring a football and sometimes whatever came to hand, such as an old ration tin. The battle honours of the German 133rd Saxon Regiment proudly records that they won their match 3-2.

Lance Corporal Cooper of the 2nd Northamptons wrote to his girlfriend describing his own strange Christmas;

'Well dear, you asked me to let you know what kind of Christmas I had. Well I never had a merry one because we were in the trenches, but we were quite happy. Now what I am going to tell you will be hard to believe, but it is quite true. There was no firing on Christmas Day and the Germans were quite friendly with us. They even came over to our trenches and gave us cigars and cigarettes and chocolate and of course we gave them things in return. Just after one o'clock on Christmas morning I was on look-out duty and one of the Germans wished me good morning and a Merry Christmas. I was never more surprised in my life when daylight came to see them all sitting on top of the trenches waving their hands and singing to us...'

An anonymous soldier, writing to the Letters Page of the Whitehaven News, recalled:

'On Christmas Eve at four p.m. we had orders that unless

the "enemy" advanced we were not to fire, and the same applied to Christmas Day. Whether the Germans had the same order or not I don't know but no shot was fired on either side. In Christmas Eve we shouted "Compliments of the Season" to each other, and passed pleasant remarks. We sang the "Austrian Anthem" and they replied with "God Save the King." On Christmas Day after service in the trenches, we went halfway and we shook hands, and had a fine crack with them. Quite a number of them speak English. I got one's autograph and he got mine, and I exchanged a button with another, and exchanged cigs and got cigars galore. Altogether we spent a very pleasant two hours with them, and found them a nice lot of fellows.'

It's believed on that magical first Christmas of 1914, the truce was respected and honoured by a full 2/3rds of the British forces. Allied commanders were of course horrified – and tried to prevent a repeat of peace breaking out during Christmas 1915 by organising artillery barrages and small scale raids against German lines just to wreck the festivities. Despite that, men from both sides still met – albeit hurriedly – in No Man's Land to exchange gifts and greetings on Christmas Eve and there were a couple of football matches played, including one spectacular match described as at least 50-a-side. By Christmas 1916, there was no more thought of peace and goodwill to all men. The horrors of gas warfare and the industrial-scale carnage on the Somme and Verdun had hardened the hearts of men.

Originally containing chocolates and cigarettes, given by Princess Mary to all servicemen in France for Christmas 1914. |
ABOVE: Fraternising of troops in Belgium on Christmas Day 1914. Group of German soldiers with two English soldiers.

The Archduke Franz Ferdinand. Not long after, the Duke and Duchess were dead. 28th June 1914.

German soldiers show the rats they caught in the trenches.

Dead French soldiers are pictured in a trench near Mareuil between Montdidier and Noyon.

British Northumberland (Hussars) Yeomanry 7th Division and German officers in No Mans Land during the unofficial truce, Christmas 1914.

'Oh what a life, living in a trench
Under Johnny French in the old French trench
We haven't got a wife or a nice little wench,
But we're still alive in the old French trench'

BEF marching song, 1915

At the start of 1915, the entire Western Front was in stalemate. For their part, the Germans were largely content to dig in hard, sit back and consolidate their gains. They had taken most of Belgium and a large slice of northern France. They were already busy at work exploiting the new industrial and mineral wealth they had captured, as well as looting valuable artefacts and machinery. Slave labourers were already being rounded up to serve the German war machine. They also needed time to think. The Schlieffen Plan had failed and grand new plans were necessary. There was a heavy demand for both men and munitions on the Eastern Front. They simply did not have the resources to crack the enemy.

To the French, and their British and Belgium allies, the situation at the start of 1915 was simply not acceptable. The French wanted the Germans out of their territory. The Belgians wanted their nation back, and the British could not abide the idea of a Western Europe increasingly dominated by the Hun. It was the Allies who were therefor motivated by the need to attack and to break the deadlock. They were the ones who were going to have to go 'over the top' —if they could only muster the forces necessary. In just a few months, the French Army had losses totalling 855,000 men. The BEF, for all its heroics at Ypres, had all but been destroyed now as a fighting force of any size. Because of lack of capacity at home, by spring they would be ordered not to expend more than a few rifle rounds per day.

The Germans had one more idea they were eager to try. They thought it might be possible to knock Britain out of the war by the twin strategy of terrorising its citizens and cutting off vital supplies coming in by sea. The German Imperial Navy had already attacked the British mainland, first at Great Yarmouth and then in December 1914, when their ships shelled Scarborough, Whitby and Hartlepool. 86 civilians and 7 soldiers had been killed in Hartlepool alone. Now over the night of 19-20th December, giant German Zeppelin airships roamed free over the Norfolk towns of King's Lynn and Great Yarmouth, dropping bombs and killing four people. They had meant to bomb Humberside but had become lost. By May 1915 German airships would be striking against London, with little the home defences could do to stop them.

On 4th February 1915, the Germans declared that they were officially blockading the sea lanes around the British Isles and both Allied and neutral shipping would be declared fair game. On May 7th, an American cargo ship was sunk off the Scilly Isles. Just six days later, a U-boat sank the British liner Lusitania off the coast of Ireland. 1,201 men, women and children died, including 128 American citizens. In the US, there was utter outrage and the whole prospect of American neutrality was threatened. Germany began to have serious second thoughts about its submarine war and on September 1st pledged that no more neutral ships would be targeted.

Italian dirigles bombing Turkish positions on Libyan Territory four years before in 1911.

Handley Page 0/400 bomber under construction.

Maurice Farman S.7 Longhorn two seat reconnaissance and training biplane.

AIR POWER

Contrary to popular belief, aircraft had already seen combat and war service prior to 1914. In 1911-12, the Italians had deployed them against the Ottoman Empire forces in Libya. Not including balloons and airships, powered flight was barely a decade odd and although these aircraft were flimsy and primitive contraptions they more than proved their worth. They provided important reconnaissance information and were actually used to drop bombs on the enemy – an improvisation dreamed up all by himself by Lieutenant Giulio Gavotti. It was a foretaste of things to come. A year later the Bulgarians dropped bombs onto Edime during the First Balkan War.

In 1914, there was still some scepticism of the true value of aircraft, even when used for reconnaissance. However, doubts were very soon dispelled. Aircraft reconnaissance over Mons helped the BEF to avoid becoming surrounded by advancing German forces and flights over the Marne allowed Allied commanders to see and exploit vulnerabilities in the positions of the German armies. Reconnaissance extended soon to artillery spotting duties, with a crude Morse code wireless device being rigged up in the cockpit.

Many of the first pilots to see action were aristocrats or wealthy businessmen from their respective countries who had learned to fly privately as a hobby. To begin with, opposing pilots would exchange friendly waves and greetings as they passed. This lasted a few months at best. Now, rival pilots were throwing rocks, grenades and even grappling hooks at each other, which progressed to firing pistols. Just three months into the war, a French aviator took a machine gun up with him.

The evolution of the aircraft into a fighting machine was astoundingly rapid. By 1915, both sides had 'scouts' - aircraft with machine guns designed for the sole purpose of shooting down enemy reconnaissance planes. That same year, Germany shocked everyone with an aircraft mounted with a machine gun synchronised to fire forward through the propeller blades of the aeroplane. It proved lethal and what became known as the 'Fokker Scourge' began - with Allied aircraft being torn from the skies wherever the Germans deployed their new fighter. It took until 1916 for the Allies to regain their mastery of the sky, with first better fighter aircraft and then specialised models which could also shoot forward through the propeller. By the time of the Battle of Verdun, the Fokker Scourge had effectively been neutralised.

The Germans regained the initiative with their D-type fighters by the end of 1916 and once again were causing heavy Allied losses until new Allied scout fighters like the Sopwith Camel and the SE5 proved a match for the Ds.

There was equal eagerness to develop aircraft capable of bombing. Using air power to drop bombs began almost soon as soon as the war started. A Zeppelin had bombed Liege on 6th August 1914 and the French bombed the Zeppelin hangers at Metz-Frascaty as early as 14th August. By 19th January 1915, German Zeppelins were dropping bombs on Norfolk, switching targets to the politically sensitive London after French bombers had attacked Berlin.

The first bombs were dropped by hand, and aimed by guesswork. The war saw the development of specialist bombsights and developments of large, purpose built bombers. The British had their Handley Page 0/400 and the Germans the Gotha, after Zeppelins proved too slow, expensive – and incendiary. Bombing strikes might be against trench lines or against cities, and it was only the weight limitations of the bomb load that prevented aerial bombardment from becoming a more decisive factor in the conflict.

Air power grew rapidly on both sides. In 1914, the Royal Flying Corps could muster a bare 63 aeroplanes. By 1919, the newly formed Royal Air Force had a fleet of 22,000 aircraft. Air power did not decide the outcome of the war, but it did become an ever-more important factor on the battlefield as the war progressed.

THE CHAMPAGNE OFFENSIVE

On 16th February 1915, an impatient Joffre launched a major French offensive against German lines in the Champagne area. The battleground was foul and sodden with winter rains and the weather equally unforgiving. The French attacked without sufficient artillery support, ploughing headlong into German defences barely scratched by the bombardment. The French also made the mistake of massing their forces in narrow corridors, making them particularly vulnerable to artillery strikes and fire from German machine gun nests.

After a month of fighting, and casualties almost reaching a quarter of a million, the French abandoned the offensive and

How to operate the "Gotha" German bomber.

German soldiers on the move near **Champagne**.

General Nivelle.

Colonel Edward Frank Harrison, chemist and inventor of the gas mask.

largely returned to their starting point. The Germans lost just 45,000 men. It was an early and painful lesson for the Allies that massed assaults against German lines could not and would not work.

NEUVE CHAPELLE

On 10th March 1915, it was the turn of the BEF to go over the top and attempt to break through German lines, supported by a strong contingent of Dominion troops from India. Field Marshal French had become concerned about the moral of the BEF languishing in their trenches and decided they ought to have something to do.

The attack centred on the village of Neuve Chapelle, in the Artois district of the Somme and achieved some degree of surprise. German defences there were weak. Events began with a 35 minute artillery bombardment from 342 British guns and the British and Indian forces soon achieved a small breakthrough in the enemy lines. Having done this, however, they were stuck and not able to advance much further. Instead they hung on, repulsing a German counter-attack some 12,000 strong. But their position was parlous. The telephone system had broken down, making effective artillery support next to impossible. Artillery support was also severely compromised by a shortage of shells – a common theme in battles to come. 1,000 Allied troops nevertheless decided to press on to assault positions at Aubers, which had not received any suppressing artillery fire. Not one of them returned alive. Support troops were eventually sent forward but these were hit by their own artillery as they advanced and beat a hasty retreat. Without proper artillery support, after three days, the victorious troops clinging on to their captured German positions had to be recalled back to their own lines having taken around 10,000 casualties. The Germans suffered similar losses.

Another lesson was learned. It might be possible to punch small, temporary holes in the enemy's defensive lines, but holding those gains and actually building from them was proving all but impossible. Joffre sadly reflected that Neuve Chapelle was, '*a success that had led to nothing*'.

More important still, the shortage of British artillery shells, noted with some fury by Sir John French, led to the fall of the British Liberal government within months. The BEF field artillery had expended 30% of its ammunition in the first day

of the Neuve Chapelle offensive. Without more shells, they could not take advantage of the BEF and Dominion soldiers' bravery and sacrifice and extend the front. Everything was for nothing.

THE SECOND BATTLE OF YPRES

'Far far from Ypres I long to be,
Where German snipers can't snipe at me
Damp is my dug-out,
Cold are my feet,
Waiting for whizz-bangs
To send me to sleep.'

British marching song.

New German military Chief of Staff Erich von Falkenhayn desperately wanted to have a 1915 offensive of his own, but since troops were so much in demand on the Eastern Front, he limited his own ambition to a strike in Flanders, aided by a new and terrible secret weapon. For the very first time, poison gas was about to be deployed and used on the Western Front.

As the German 4th Army assaulted French positions around the Belgian town of Ypres, it used some 5,000 canisters to deploy clouds of poisonous green chlorine gas against the Allies. The target of the gas assault was two French Moroccan and Algerian forces. Whether the Germans deliberately chose them because they were African and not white is still a matter of some debate. In releasing the gas, the Germans were entirely at the mercy of the wind. When the gas blew back at them, many of the gas operators died too or were horrifically injured. The French forces, which were not equipped with any protection, were smothered by over 170 tons of pure poison. There were 6,000 casualties. Many choked to death. Others went blind. The survivors fell back in panic and a five mile gap in the Allied lines swiftly opened up. However, the Germans were very slow to enter the breach as they too were terrified of their own gas clouds. Canadian troops rushed to fill the gap temporarily, being able to partly negate the effects of the gas by urinating into cloths and tying them around their faces.

Neuve Chapelle aftermath.

Poster showing soldiers in battle at **Neuve-Chapelle,** designed and lithographed by **Frank Brangwyn.**

Second Battle of Ypres, 22 April to May 1915 by Richard Jack.

Aftermath of the fighting in the French town of **Carency** during the **Second Battle of Artois, May 1915.**

French TNH-type gas mask, made in 1915-16.

They took ferocious losses as the Germans finally summoned up their nerve and came in for the kill. It was here, a Canadian historian said that their brave behaviour in holding the line *'set the standard for the Canadian Army that was to be'.*

An eyewitness to the first chlorine gas attack, Lance Sergeant Elmer Cotton, provided a vivid description of its effect:

'It produces a flooding of the lungs – it is an equivalent death to drowning only on dry land. The effects are these – a splitting headache and terrific thirst (to drink water is instant death), a knife edge of pain in the lungs and the coughing up of a greenish froth off the stomach and the lungs, ending finally in insensibility and death. The colour of the skin from white turns a greenish black and yellow, the colour protrudes and the eyes assume a glassy stare. It is a fiendish death to die.'

Private W. Hay of the Royal Scots arrived in Ypres just after the chlorine gas attack on 22 April 1915:

'We knew there was something that was wrong. We started to march towards Ypres but we couldn't get past on the road with refugees coming down the road. We went along the railway line to Ypres and there were people, civilians and soldiers, lying along the roadside in a terrible state. We heard them say it was gas. We didn't know what the hell gas was. When we got to Ypres we found a lot of Canadians lying there dead from gas the day before, poor devils, and it was quite a horrible sight for us young men. I was only twenty so it was quite traumatic and I've never forgotten nor ever will forget it'

French and British troops fell back to well-prepared secondary lines of defence and the town stayed in Allied hands but the Germans did make some significant advances, using gas several more times. Fighting raged from 21st April to 25th May. The Allies suffered some 58,000 casualties, the Germans 38,000. Ten VCs were won during the action.

ARTOIS AND VIMY RIDGE

By April 1915, the war in the East was going badly for the Russians. They desperately needed more pressure to be applied to German forces on the Western Front, draining them of weapons, shells and men that could otherwise be used on the Eastern Front. Allied commanders on the Western Front understood their plight – and launched a late Spring offensive.

On 3rd May, the French commenced a shattering six day, thousand gun artillery barrage against German trenches in the Artois. As the guns fell silent, the French 6th Army went over the top, breached the battered German lines and seized the strategically important target of Vimy Ridge. Once there though, they could advance no further and there were insufficient reserves and resources available to help them capitalise on their hard-won gains. The very next day, a determined German counter-attack drove them from the ridge and sent them spilling back towards their own lines.

As the French launched their attack on Vimy Ridge, British and Indian troops made a second strike around what was left of the village of Neuve Chapelle in the Artois. The attack was a disaster. The British possessed nowhere near enough artillery shells to sufficiently damage the German defensive line. As a result, the troops were decimated by machine gun fire as they advanced. The attack was swiftly abandoned at the cost of 11,000 casualties.

The British and Indians tried again, on 15th May , attacking Festubert, north of Neuve Chapelle. This time a 60 hour artillery bombardment was laid down on German positions before the Allies went over the top. It didn't help. The British and Indian troops managed to get just 1,000 yards – just over half a mile – and took 16,000 casualties for that slimmest of gains.

On 16th June, the French once again tried to seize Vimy Ridge, walking into the most ferocious of German artillery barrages as they advanced. They reached the ridge against all odds and took it – only to lose it once more to a powerful German counter attack the very next day. After suffering 100,000 dead, wounded and missing the French finally cancelled the offensive.

Indian infantry in the trenches, prepared against a **gas attack**.

Poison gas attack.

LOOS AND CHAMPAGNE – THE 'BIG PUSH'

The great Autumn Offensive of 1915 started in earnest on 15th September, with the French going over the top to attack Champagne. *'Your elan will be irresistible!'* Joffre told his men. Simultaneously, British forces concentrated on Loos in the Artois and launched their single largest offensive of the year.

The British had wanted to postpone the offensive until 1916 to build up men and munitions but Joffre wanted results now. His was the country that was invaded and, as the British were very much the junior partners in the war, they would have to fall in line with his wishes.

Squadrons of the Royal Flying Corps flew missions to bomb German-held railway lines and other communications, in addition providing artillery spotting and reconnaissance support. Yet again there were not enough artillery shells for the British guns to lay down a truly effective bombardment. It was now that British troops launched their first ever gas attack of the war, with the Royal Engineers emptying 5,000 cylinders of chlorine gas in the direction of the German trench line. British soldiers rolled in behind, respirators on and bayonets at the ready. They discovered that those Germans not already poisoned to death had fled, leaving a four mile hole in their lines. The British paused at Loos, suffering from a lack of supplies, reserves and from the seemingly inevitable communications problems with HQ. When they resumed their attack the next day they met a determined line of German resistance beyond the town, with fortifications bristling with machine guns. The advancing British were cut to pieces. One observer in the field later wrote:

'From what I can ascertain, some of the divisions did actually reach the enemy's trenches, for their bodies can now be seen on the barbed wire.'

When the finally tally was made, 50,000 British troops were dead, wounded or missing. It was the final straw for the British government. Sir John French was fired as commander of the British Army and General Sir Douglas Haig promoted in his place. French had become increasingly disillusioned by the trench war, and horrified by his losses. He had lost all real enthusiasm – but Haig was altogether a different proposition. A dour, quiet Scot from a wealthy whisky family, he was prepared to wage total war whatever the cost. He would, in the bloody months and years to come, display the true tenacious British Bulldog spirit – or a terrifying inability to learn from experience – perhaps both.

While the British were fighting in Loos, a simultaneous French assault by their 2nd Army had expertly exploited a weakness in the German lines and punched a hole some three miles deep and six miles wide. As they paused to try and work out what to do with their gains, they were hit full on by a massed counter-attack by the German 3rd Army. Plagued by a chronic lack of ammunition, they were forced to retreat once more. As the gunfire ceased, 145,000 French soldiers were dead or wounded. A separate assault on Vimy Ridge did however finally succeed in securing the tactically vital area for the French. **This time they held it.**

British soldiers loading a battery of Livens gas projectors. Taken at Royal Engineers Experimental Station, **Porton, UK.**
ABOVE: English gas bomb 1915.

Tethered balloon, with observers from the artillery. In the summer of 1915 in Lorraine.

German Gotha WD II 1915 120 hp Mercedes engine.

The german armoured cruiser SMS Blücher sinks after receiving multiple hits from British warships at the Battle of Dogger Bank on 25 January 1915.

Gassed by John Singer.

"A strange helper for war: An elephant, which was donated to the army by Hagenbeck, now helps behind the Western Front.".

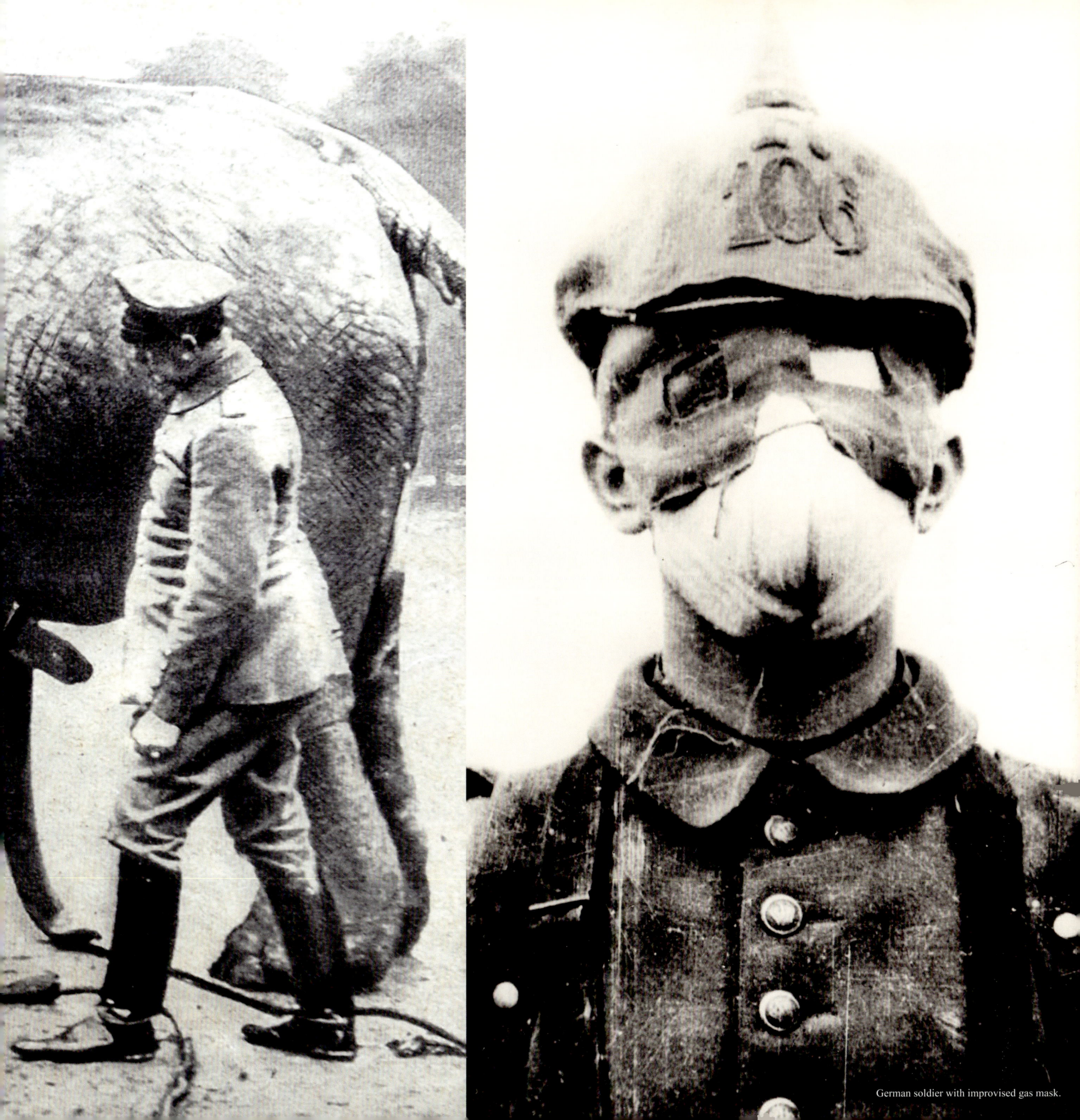

German soldier with improvised gas mask.

British soldiers in the trench.

The year began with US President Woodrow Wilson desperately trying to arrange European peace talks. He'd still be trying come December. It was a slippery path for Wilson who was facing an election year, running on the slogan, 'he kept us out of war'. In April, America threatened to sever all diplomatic ties with Germany over their U-boat campaign. In response, Germany once more backed down and declared an end to their submarine blockade of Britain. It wouldn't last.

The British and German fleets would meet in inconclusive battle at Jutland and the Germans, still determined to get around the trench lines, would supply arms and assistance to the Nationalists for the Easter rising in Dublin. A new coalition government held power in Britain, taking unprecedented measures to control civilian life to aid the war effort.

Looking back over the great offensives of 1915, senior military staff and politicians realised that, while there were a great many lessons to be learned, there were precious few answers to be found. Even if an attacking force managed to seize its objective, it was almost impossible to capitalise on the moment. Communications were poor, if they existed at all. Commanders consequently often had little idea what was going on. They could therefore not commit reserves to support the attacking force. If the enemy had defences in depth, the attacking force might find itself trying to storm positions unaffected by artillery with disastrous consequences. Battle-weary victorious forces were extremely vulnerable to swift counter-attacks, having no time to prepare defences. If they moved to take advantage of a perceived enemy weakness, they might find themselves where they weren't supposed to be on the battlefield and attacked by their own artillery. In almost every situation, the attacker was at a lethal disadvantage. Everything favoured stalemate. Artillery barrages could make a real difference, depending on their power and accuracy, but they required truly colossal amounts of munitions to be effective – and they gave away the element of surprise.

French soldiers of the **87th Regiment, 6th Division**, northwest of Verdun.

Field Marshal Paul von Hindenburg and staff.

French reserves crossing a river on the way to **Verdun**.

CONCRIPTION

*'If you want to find the old battalion,
I know where they are
They're hanging on the old barbed wire.'*

from a British marching song

As the true horrors of war on the Western Front became more apparent during late 1914 and early 1915, the numbers of Britons volunteering for Kitchener's New Army began to dry up. Even social pressure and women giving white feathers to men who didn't volunteer could not drive enough men into the recruiting office any more. There was only one last solution – conscription. Eventually over 2,700,000 British men would be fed to the war effort this way.

The Military Service Act was passed in January 1916 and came into effect in March, requiring men between the ages of 18 and 41 to be called up for military service. Originally married men were exempt from conscription but this was changed very quickly after the true death toll on the Somme started to become apparent. As the number of fatalities soared, the upper age limit for conscription rose to 51 years old and it became harder and harder to get an exemption based on work of national importance or whatever other grounds still existed. By 1918, there was serious talk of conscripting even clergymen to fight.

Britain needed every warm body it could get.

THE BATTLE OF VERDUN

'Ils ne passeront pas' (They shall not pass)

General Henri-Philippe Petain.

One commander who understood the lessons of 1915 all too well was the Chief of the German General Staff, Erich von Falkenhayn. He had told the Kaiser that there was just no prospect of a German offensive successfully breaking through Allied lines. Instead, he had a plan, based on the very failure of offensive strategies. Using this plan – which he called

'Operation Judgement' - he would, he said, *'bleed France white'*. Three Frenchmen would die for every German, he promised. He was about to ignite the biggest battle the world had ever known.

Verdun was a small city on the Meuse River to the north east of France, ringed by a double ringed network of 28 defensive forts. It also occupied a special place in the French psyche and so, Falkenhayn reasoned, they would never be prepared to see it surrendered to the Germans, no matter what the price of defending it. Falkenhayn's plan, therefore, was to capture the Meuse Heights overlooking the city, heavily fortify their position and then bring up the big guns. They would mass their artillery, which would include so-called 'super guns' like 'Big Bertha', feed them with shells from a nearby railway network, and then subject Verdun to unprecedented bombardment. Falkenhayn then expected the French to try and regain the Meuse Heights at any and all cost, storming well-fortified defensive positions uphill in the teeth of withering machine gun and artillery fire. The French losses would be colossal, he predicted. They might expend their entire reserve dashing themselves frantically against the Heights. Also working in Falkenhayn's favour, Verdun was in a Salient with the Germans effectively controlling three sides of a square around it – and its massive forts had been weakened by Joffre to provide men, guns and munitions for use elsewhere on the Western Front. The whole operation, said Falkenhayn, should take just a matter of weeks.

The French had some notion of what Falkenhayn was attempting to do, thanks to information provided by the supposedly neutral Dutch military intelligence, but were far too slow to act upon it. Bad weather held up the launch of the German assault until 21st February, but when it came 140,000 men of Falkenhayn's 5th Army initially made rapid advances on the east bank of the river and one of the city forts, Douaumont, was captured without a shot being fired. This stunned the French. Douaumont was reputed to be the toughest fort in the world. In reality it was manned by just 56 amateur pensioners who readily gave themselves up. With the fall of Douaumont, Verdun was now just five miles away.

The attack was supported by a massive – and devastating - artillery barrage from 1,200 guns. 100,000 shells an hour landed on the French lines. The shell fire was of an intensity men had never seen before. It has been estimated that 2,400 shells would fall on each area the size of a football pitch. One French eyewitness described its effects thus:

'Men were squashed. Cut in two or divided from top to bottom. Blown into showers; bellies turned inside out; skulls

MILITARY SERVICE ACT, 1916

Every man to whom the Act applies will on Thursday, March 2nd, be deemed to have enlisted for the period of the War unless he is excepted or exempt.

Any man who has adequate grounds for applying to a Local Tribunal for a

CERTIFICATE OF EXEMPTION UNDER THIS ACT

Must do so **BEFORE**

THURSDAY, MARCH 2

Why wait for the Act to apply to you?
Come now and join of your own free will.
You can at once put your claim for exemption from being called up before a Local Tribunal if you wish.

ATTEST NOW

Military service act poster.

The Crown Prince of Germany on the Verdun front, giving Iron Crosses to men who have distinguished themselves for valor.

General Von Falkenhayn.

General Charles Mangin.

forced into the chest as if by a blow from a club.'

Falkenhayn had expected the French to fight more ferociously for the east bank. Instead, they took the opportunity to build in depth defences and committed over 20 divisions to the defence of the west bank of the Meuse. Newly promoted General Philippe Petain gave orders to hold the line at all costs and even to launch harassing attacks against the massing German forces on the east bank, while French artillery constantly kept them under bombardment.

Petain – like Falkenhayn - was an advocate of defensive fighting and knew that, if he could force the Germans to expend themselves attacking, he could do a lot of damage. Already, German losses were far exceeding those anticipated by Falkenhayn. March saw renewed offensives by the Germans on the west bank with only partial success. Simultaneous attacks on both river banks in April along a 20 mile wide front again resulted in only partial success for the Germans and were only gained by heavy losses. Falkenhayn had planned a battle of attrition to wear down the French forces but now he was finding his own forces being relentlessly ground down too. German losses in April were not much short of French losses. Everyone was trapped in the meat grinder.

French troops were rotated more frequently than the men of the German 5th and were therefore fresher and less exhausted. Three quarters of the men in the French Army would take their turn to serve at Verdun. French morale did not collapse as Falkenhayn had hoped and indeed was lifted by defending such an important city. Nevertheless, he persevered. He was committed - and trapped.

The battlefield by May was sodden with rain and resembled a carpet of clinging mud filled with shattered human remains. Deep shell craters were filled with liquid filth in which any man unfortunate enough to take shelter or fall in would very probably drown. Whole woods were reduced to stumps and splinters. Roads simply disappeared. Outlying towns and villages dissolved into smouldering piles or shattered timber and pulverised brick. Many have still not been rebuilt or repaired to this day and scar the French countryside providing poignant and perhaps permanent memorials.

One French artillery officer, later to be killed, confided in his diary:

'Humanity is mad. It must be mad to do what it is doing. What a massacre! What scenes of horror and carnage! I cannot find words to translate my impressions. Hell cannot be so terrible. Men are mad!'

The long awaited breakthrough for the German 5th Army began at the start of May 1916, when a concerted attack along the west bank finally broke through and seized two strategically important hills from the French. The Germans pressed on and took Fort Vaux before finally seizing the Meuse Heights they had set out to capture all the way back in February. From a position of strength they now swept on to attack Fort Souville which protected some strategically vital bridges over the Meuse and took the nearby town of Fleury, which they assaulted using Phosgene gas. A new horror, Phosgene gas turned into hydrochloric acid when inhaled into the lungs. It was ten times more lethal than Chlorine gas. 110,000 gas shells were fired at the French – but the Germans were now stopped dead in their tracks by a huge French counter-attack, just two miles from Verdun itself. On July 10th, using gas once more, the German 5th Army again tried to take Fort Souville only to be repulsed once more.

Now with the Somme offensive underway to the west, Falkenhayn had to spare troops to meet a fresh Allied assault and could not put the kind of strength he wanted behind his offensive in Verdun. A simultaneous offensive mounted by the Russians on the eastern front put further strain on the supply of men and munitions to the increasingly threadbare 5th Army. As a result, German soldiers were asked to be sparing with their ammunition.

The Battle of Verdun was not going the way Falkenhayn had promised. German losses were savage, Instead of being the defenders, the Germans were too frequently on the offensive and getting chewed to pieces by the defending French. Above everything, Falkenhayn had severely underestimated the French. On 28th August, a less-than-impressed Kaiser dismissed Falkenhayn for his failures and replaced him with Field Marshal Paul von Hindenburg and his second-in-command, Erich Ludendorff. They would effectively run the war for the Kaiser from now on, while Falkenhayn was despatched to the Transylvanian Front for his sins. Hindenburg would be the grand figurehead, while Ludendorff would plan and fight the battles.

On 10th October, the French under Robert Nivelle finally took the initiative. Although recognised as a national hero for his defence of Verdun, Petain was a defensive thinker and he was promoted away from the battlefield. Nivelle was a more offensive general, and in his task he was given the services of General Mangin, a man who had earned the nickname of 'The Butcher'. Nivelle was an artilleryman by profession and took full advantage of his expertise. He launched his offensive along the east bank to recapture Fort Douaumont

Portrait of Philippe Pétain.

French long gun battery overrun by the German forces at **Verdun.**

Sir Douglas Haig.

A Royal Flying Corps observer demonstrates a **C type** aerial reconnaissance camera fixed to the side of the fuselage.

General Sir Henry Seymour Rawlinson.

with the largest artillery barrage the French had yet unleashed in the war. He also tried a new tactic, the 'creeping barrage', with his troops slowly advancing just behind an artillery bombardment that constantly moved forward as the troops did. French forces succeeded in retaking Fort Douaumont, before seizing Fort Vaux just over a week later. Three days later, the French finally drove the German forces clear of the strategic area surrounding Verdun and the battle effectively came to an end. Because of his success at Verdun Nivelle would replace Joffre as Commander –in-Chief of the French Army on 12th December.

Raging from 21st February to 15th December 1916, Verdun was more than just the longest battle in the First World War. It was also the longest battle in history – and one of the most costly. The opposing armies had expended in the region of 10 million artillery shells against each other, some from the biggest guns and mortars on the planet. It's widely reported that men died or went mad from the shelling without ever seeing an enemy soldier to raise arms against. One French soldier described the effect of an oncoming artillery barrage thus:

'When you hear the whistling in the distance your entire body preventively crunches together to prepare for the enormous explosions. Every new explosion is a new attack, a new fatigue, a new affliction. Even nerves of the hardest of steel, are not capable of dealing with this kind of pressure. The moment comes when the blood rushes to your head, the fever burns inside your body and the nerves, numbed with tiredness, are not capable of reacting to anything anymore.'

Another said:

'There is nothing as tiring as the continuous, enormous bombardment as we have lived through, last night, at the front. The night is disturbed by light as clear as if it were day. The earth moves and shakes like jelly. And the men who are still at the frontline, cannot hear anything but the drumfire, the moaning of wounded friends, the screams of hurt horses, the wild pounding of their own hearts, hour after hour, day after day, night after night....'

Some men said they were quite

desperate to be shot to death and therefore have something for their family to bury, rather than being reduced to pulp mingled with earth. Another horror of war, the flamethrower, was widely used by German units for the first time. One French soldier recalled the aftermath:.

'...At my feet two unlucky creatures rolled the floor in misery. Their clothes and hands, their entire bodies were on fire. They were living torches. (The next day) in front of us on the floor the two I had witnessed ablaze, lay rattling. They were so unrecognisably mutilated that we could not decide on their identities. Their skin was black entirely. One of them died that same night. In a fit of insanity the other hummed a tune from his childhood, talked to his wife and his mother and spoke of his village. Tears were in our eyes....'

At the height of the horror, at least one French unit tried to desert and flee across all of France to take refuge in neutral Spain. Those apprehended were shot at dawn. The French suffered over 370,000 casualties and the Germans almost 340,000 casualties. 100,000 of those who died at Verdun have never been found.

PLANNING THE SOMME OFFENSIVE

'The machine gun is a most overrated weapon… The way to capture machine guns is by grit and determination'

General Sir Douglas Haig, 1915

There had always been a major Allied offensive planned for 1916. Haig wanted it centred on Flanders, where he thought he could liberate large slices of Belgium and end the use of Belgian ports as home for U-boat raiders. He was overruled by Joffre, who favoured the Somme to the east. After the surprise German attack at Verdun, it was agreed to carry on with the offensive, but with significant changes. The plan now was to draw German reserves from Verdun and provide some much-needed relief to the beleaguered French forces there. With the French so committed at Verdun, it was also decided that the British forces would constitute the bulk

8-inch howitzers of the **39th Siege Battery, Royal Garrison Artillery** in the **Fricourt-Mametz Valley**.

Men of the Royal Garrison Artillery in **Englebelmer Wood** moving a **15-inch Howitzer shell.**

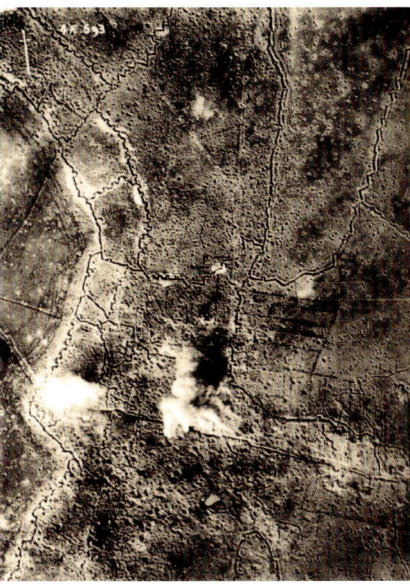

Aerial photograph of **Thiepval village, Somme**, and German front-line and support trenches, while undergoing bombardment by British artillery.

of the troops taking part. Only Haig thought that the offensive could achieve more than being a mere diversion. He believed that the Germans would break, given sufficient pressure, and the Somme could actually lead to a major breakthrough on the Western Front.

Haig suggested 15th August as a possible starting date for the offensive at which point, he recalls in his war diaries, 'Joffre at once got very excited and shouted that '*the French army would cease to exist then if we did nothing til then.''* Haig dearly wanted to play for time. He thought his 'New Army' – Kitchener's Mob of volunteers - wasn't ready for the task. However he understood Joffre's point of view: The French had suffered over 200,000 casualties at Verdun by late May of 1916. Haig compromised. The Somme Offensive would be brought forward to 1st July.

British troops would be charged with assaulting a 15 mile front between Serre and Curlu, with General Sir Henry Rawlinson commanding 4th Army forces in the North and General Allenby in the South of operations with elements of the 3rd Army. Five French divisions from the 6th Army, meanwhile would simultaneously strike at eight miles of German lines stretching from Peronne to Curlu. After the initial assault by British infantry, it was planned that they would be rapidly reinforced by massed British cavalry galloping across No Man's Land. Haig was an ex-Hussar and a cavalry enthusiast, and could still envisage cavalry being effective on the modern battlefield, a view shared by very few others at the time.

The British Army forces preparing to go 'over the top' now were very different from the experienced, professional soldiers the BEF had fielded in 1914. A few survivors of the 'Old Contemptibles' still remained, but the bulk of troops assembled were from Kitchener's New Army, the men who had volunteered with such passion and pride to serve the nation. They were amateurs, civilians, largely untested in battle. Here were the 'Pals Battalions'. They faced battle-hardened German soldiers, many of whom had just been rotated out of Verdun.

THE SOMME – THE OPENING BARRAGE

The Somme Offensive opened on 24th June 1916 with a week-long artillery barrage directed against German positions, during which a staggering 1, 738,000 rounds were fired. It was the largest artillery barrage the world had ever known and it's claimed that, at its height, it could be heard as far away as Hampstead Heath in North London. Sir Henry Rawlinson told his officers with complete confidence:

'*...nothing could exist at the conclusion of the bombardment in the area covered by it.'*

What he did not know was that the barrage had been far less effective than anticipated. The German positions were four storeys deep in place, often protected by reinforced concrete and were far from having been obliterated. Only a direct hit could have killed the men inside and many shells had been off target. The British also fired far too many shrapnel rounds rather than high explosive ordnance. Shrapnel rounds might prove devastating against relatively unprotected troops, but were almost useless against barbed wire, men underground or in bunkers. Haig had also insisted that the bombardment should be spread across both the first and second lines of German defences, thereby 'thinning out' the effect of the bombardment. Later, it was also discovered that as many as one third of the rounds had failed to explode. Even today, farmers on the Somme are still discovering huge quantities of unexploded munitions from that bombardment. The ferocious barbed wire entanglements, as broad as 40 yards in places and as thick as a man's finger were still largely intact. The British commanders simply had no idea that their barrage had been so ineffective. It was inconceivable. But it was also a fact. The night before battle commenced, Haig wrote to his wife. In his letter he said:

'*I feel that every step in my plan has been taken with the Divine help...The wire has never been so well cut, nor the artillery preparation so thorough....'*

THE FIRST DAY OF THE SOMME

Just before 7.30 am on 1st July 1916, seventeen huge explosions were seen in the German defensive positions as Allied mines were detonated. British sappers had tunnelled under the battlefield and had planted enormous amounts of explosives literally under the German's feet. It was an impressive and cheering sight to the thousands of soldiers waiting in the British lines, but it wouldn't be nearly enough.

General Allenby.

British Gunners firing an 18 pounder gun at **St Leger aux Boise.**

British Vickers machine gun crew wearing **PH-type anti-gas** helmets. Near **Ovillers** during **The Battle of the Somme.**

At 7.30 in the morning, whistles started blowing in the British trenches to signal the start of the offensive. Fourteen British Divisions went 'over the top' in waves along an 18 mile front and started walking slowly towards the German lines, supported by a creeping barrage.

They were told to walk slowly, lined up shoulder-to-shoulder, in perfect parade ground extended line formations towards the enemy. The idea had come from Rawlinson, whose background was in the infantry. Haig had wanted the men to fight forward in small groups working in sympathy with the terrain and the cover, but Rawlinson thought that this sort of tactic was beyond the still-green recruits of Kitchener's Army. They would have a better understanding of manoeuvres practiced on the parade ground than the battlefield.

The average soldier was laden down with over 60 lbs of equipment, including two sandbags per man for shoring up defences later. Each rifleman carried the standard 150 rounds of ammunition, with many carrying extra in bandoliers slung over their shoulders. They were expected to swiftly take their objectives and then dig in and hang on until literally, they would be saved by the cavalry. A private from the 1st Bradford Pals recalled:

'There was no lingering about when zero hour came. Our platoon officer blew his whistle and he was the first up the scaling ladder, with his revolver in one hand and a cigarette in the other. 'Come on, boys,' he said, and up he went. We went up after him one at a time. I never

saw the officer again.'

Confidence that the German forces had been destroyed was so high that one British captain, Billy Nevill of the 8th East Surreys, dished out soccer balls to his men and promised a prize to the first man to land one in a German trench. He was to die just short of the wire.

For their part, the German forces emerged from their deep secure bunkers, set up their machine gun nests and waited. Visibility was perfect. It was a lovely summer Saturday morning.

As the advancing British came into view, the German gunners opened up. The first wave was hit by a wall of fire that cut them to pieces. Men from the rank behind rushed forward to fill the gaps, only to fall in turn. They had been told that German resistance would be light to non-existent. Instead, they were mown down by devastatingly effective and voluminous machine gun fire from defensive positions that were assumed to have been knocked out. To add to the carnage, German artillery now opened up, splitting their fire between the extended line formations and the soldiers still waiting for orders to advance out of the assembly trenches.

The British quickly dropped the idea of advancing in waves at a slow pace. The men started to scatter, to duck down and crawl towards the enemy positions ahead of them, or dart from shell hole to shell hole. Many made it forward, only to discover that the huge entanglements of barbed wire were still largely intact ahead of them. A desperate struggle began to cut the wire and clear paths, all the while under withering machine gun fire.

One German Officer on the front line recalled:

'We rushed to the ramparts, there they come-the khaki yellows, not more than twenty metres in front of the trench. They advanced fully equipped, slowly to march across our bodies and into the open country. But no boys, we are still alive and the moles have come out of their holes...Machine gun fire tears holes in their ranks. They discover our presence; throw themselves down into the mass of craters welcomed by hand grenades and machine guns. It is their turn to sell their lives'.

All along the front, officers desperately improvised, trying a host of different tactics – sometimes to help close with the enemy, sometimes just to try and save as many men as they could. Some troops were ordered to dump their gear and fix bayonets. Some advancing forces actually reached enemy lines. Others took their objective. One of the deciding factors was how effective the preliminary artillery barrage had been in the area. Where the bombardment had worked, mainly to the south where the 3rd Army was in action, British troops

German field gun.

British infantry advancing in support during the **Battle of Morval.**

Soldiers of the **1st Battalion, The Lancashire Fusiliers** fixing bayonets prior to the attack on **Beaumont Hamel.**

German dead scattered in the wreck of a machine gun post near **Guillemont.**

made greater advances. But the barrage had been effective in far too few places. Almost everywhere else the attack stalled. Men started to stream back in retreat. Those few who had gained their objectives joined them, unable to hold with their flanks exposed.

One British witness, looking out over No-Man's Land, described the aftermath:

'Quite as many died on the enemy wire as on the ground, like fish caught in the net. They hung there in grotesque postures. Some looked as if they were praying; they had died on their knees and the wire had prevented their fall. Machine gun fire had done its terrible work.'

As streams of wounded stumbled back to their lines, stretcher bearers made desperate efforts to cope but were totally overwhelmed. One estimated that, if there had been ten times the number of stretcher bearers on hand, they would have been overwhelmed too. Men who could crawl back to safety were ordered to do so, so that the even more grievously injured could be given priority. In places, truces were hastily arranged so that expeditions could safely venture into No Man's Land to recover the wounded. Many were not reached for days and many more died of their wounds waiting for help.

60% of all British officers who took part in the assault were killed. German soldiers had been trained how to spot them and ordered to concentrate their fire on them. The casualty rate was 40% for all other ranks. In total, on that one day alone, British casualties numbered 60,000 – of whom 20,000 were killed outright. It was the single bloodiest day in the history of the British Army. Nine Victoria Crosses were won that day – all but three of them posthumous.

The French assault had been much more successful. Their relatively small artillery barrage on the morning of 1st July caught the Germans by surprise and was more effective than the British. German lines were weaker in their sector, as Falkenhayn could not envisage the French going on the offensive while still embroiled in Verdun. They made some considerable gains, but with the total failure of the British assault, they could not make good on those gains and had to fall back to their trench lines again.

THE SOMME OFFENSIVE

At home in Britain, the news of the Somme Offensive was

initially cheery and positive – but the reality soon became apparent. Whole Pals Battalions had been wiped out. Individual towns lost virtually all their young men on the same day. Postmen and telegram boys could not bear the awful job of delivering all the death notices to homes, often in the same streets. Many broke down. Others left their jobs. Something truly terrible had happened.

For several days, Haig had no idea of the full losses the British had suffered. Intelligence officers were in the habit of bringing him only the good news. He thought casualties were around 40,000 at most, which he considered acceptable given an offensive of this magnitude, and decided to carry on.

By 11th July, the German first line had been captured and Allied forces were facing the enemy's second line of defence. Within days, German reinforcements were being rushed from Verdun to stem the threat. Both sides believed the other was on the verge of collapse and the Somme settled in to a true battle of attrition. Periodically the Allies would launch offensives and draw out the Germans in an immediate counter-attack as per Falkenhayn's explicit instructions. The exposed Germans would then be subjected to everything the Allies could throw at them, resulting in huge casualties. In August the combined efforts of the French and British succeed in capturing the German second line of defence in many places – but it was a hard won and sour victory.

Also in August, the Kaiser sacked Falkenhayn for his handling both of Verdun and the Somme. Falkenhayn's plans had revolved around fewer German casualties. Instead, the German Army was haemorrhaging from its losses. Falkenhayn was replaced by Hindenburg and Ludendorff. Being another defensive thinker, one of Hindenburg's first decisions was to build a massive new line of defences to the north of present German positions. He called it the Siegfried Line – but it became better known as the Hindenburg Line. His intention was to retreat German forces on the Somme back to this line and then let the Allies smash themselves to pieces assaulting it.

On the 15th September, the British unleashed their secret weapon at the Battle of Flers-Courcelette – the tank. It was a somewhat inauspicious introduction. The earliest models proved too lightly armed and armoured, too few in number, not manoeuvrable enough and highly prone to breaking down quite abruptly. Less than half the 50 tanks supplied actually made it onto the battlefield. They did cause – not surprisingly – a great deal of shock and surprise amongst the German ranks, many

Young German soldier at **The Battle of the Somme.**

A **German prisoner helps** British wounded make their way to a dressing station near **Bernafay Wood** following fighting on **Bazentin Ridge,**

Little Willie.

Mark V Tank that didn't see action until 1918.

of whom mistook their exhaust fumes for poisonous gas dispensers - and they did turn the tide of battle in a number of places. The 15th Scottish Division took Martinpuich with the aid of just one solitary tank as did the Hampshires and Royal West Kents at Flers - Courcelette however was taken by Canadian infantry alone, as the seven tanks assigned to them couldn't keep up with the pace of their assault. Other tanks got hopelessly lost on the field of battle and, in some tragic cases, started to blast away at their own forces. Overall, less than a mile was gained in the whole 15 division assault. Nevertheless, a few days later, Haig sent word to London requesting 1,000 more tanks. He was convinced. One German officer confronted by the tanks, called them *'unearthly monsters...spewing death'*. In his later report, he could only describe them as *'extraordinary vehicles'*. No one knew the term tank – yet.

Early in October, the German 3rd line of trenches fell to the Allies and, throughout that month, Joffre vigorously encouraged Haig to keep up the pressure. The French were turning the tide at Verdun and the German forces at the Somme needed to be held in place. After more than four months of fighting and over 90 different Allied attacks on German positions – almost all of which had been met with a German counter-attack, the Somme Offensive was finally called to a halt on the 18th November 1916. Weeks of driving rain, interspersed with ferocious blizzards, had rendered the battlefield almost untraversable and fighting almost impossible.

Finally, the Allies held fast and at last decided to take score. The British had lost some 420,000 men, the French almost 200,000 and the Germans took 650,000 casualties. The offensive that had only been intended as a sideshow to Verdun had been even more bloody than Verdun, and resulted in even higher casualties. For all the fighting and for all the casualties, the Allies had only advanced their lines some seven miles. It had cost them almost 1 ½ casualties per inch of ground gained. It was however, still their biggest advance since the Marne back in 1914.

Haig declared victory, concluding in his despatch:

'Verdun had been relieved; the main German forces had been held on the Western front; and the enemy's strength had been very considerably worn down. Any one of these three results is in itself sufficient to justify the Somme battle.'

In fighting the Somme Offensive, Haig did exactly what he would do again and again on future offensives. He would press on and on, long after it made sense in the hope that, this time, the Germans would finally crack and break. This is the key to understanding Haig's tactical thinking.

Taking stock of the events of 1916, the German High Command secretly concluded that they could simply not survive another year like that...

THE TANK

The idea of a 'tank' had been around for some years before the outbreak of WWI. H.G. Wells had written about steam-powered 'Land Ironclads' in 1903 and in 1911 an Australian civil engineer had actually submitted a tank design to the British War Office. They turned him away. Peeved, he was tempted to go and offer his design (which was better than the British tank eventually produced) to the Germans – but didn't out of a sense of patriotism.

Surprisingly, the Army showed next to no interest in the concept – and the first British tanks were developed by the Royal Navy instead, on the instigation of Winston Churchill, who was at the time First Lord of the Admiralty.

The Royal Navy produced their first tank, 'Little Willie' in September 1915 and rapidly developed an improved version which could successfully cross trenches, nicknamed 'Mother' or 'Big Willie' . This would become the standard template for the first battle tanks. Two versions were made – a 'male' which was armed with cannon and machine guns and a 'female' which was more lightly armed with just machine guns. Each carried a crew of eight – four of whom were needed to steer or work the gears.

They were called 'tanks' because of their resemblance to the steel water tanks at the manufacturing plant. The Navy wanted to call them 'Land Ships' but the name 'tank' stuck, partly because it helped the secrecy of the project. Someone

British **Mark I** tank at **The Battle of the Somme**.

An early model British **Mark I** "male" tank, named **C-15**, near **Thiepval**.

might guess what a 'land ship' was, but a 'tank'..?

Although mechanically unreliable and vulnerable to determined enemy fire, almost 2,600 tanks were eventually deployed by the British Army before the end of the war. The French tank was developed quite separately at about the same time and featured a traversable turret – a design feature which is standard on tanks to the present day. Over 3,000 were built.

Germany, having observed the unreliability and vulnerability of the tank on the battlefield, gravely underestimated its importance. It was seen as ridiculous in some quarters and a novelty in others. Because of this, the Germans were very slow to come up with a tank of their own. The A7V was eventually developed – but only 20 were ever built before the end of the war. The Germans also had around 35 captured British tanks which they pressed into service to support their troops.

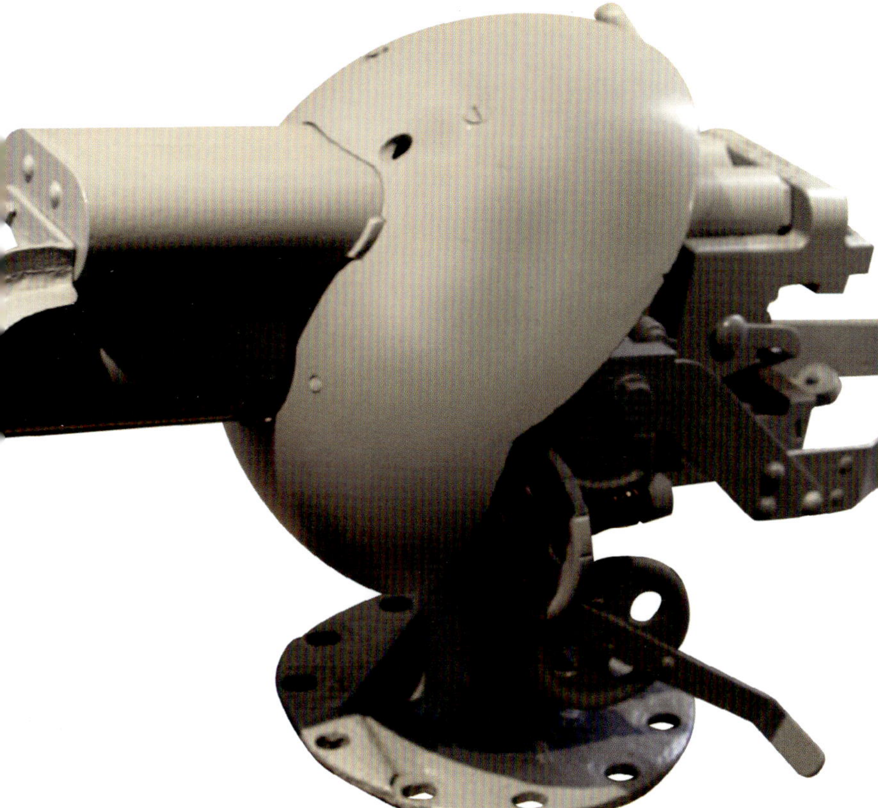

Hornsby & Sons tractor with **'chain-track**.
ABOVE: Captured British tanks being transported by rail.
LEFT: Blockhaus Schneider 75 mm tank gun.

Soccer team of British soldiers with gas masks.

Canadians making an attack, leaving trenches on the Somme.

A ration party of the Royal Irish Rifles in a communication trench during the Battle of the Somme.

1st Lancashire Fusiliers tending their wounded in the trenches during the Battle of Albert.

Canadian troops going "over the top" during training near St Pol, France.

German soldiers with a captured British Mark IV series tank, converted for German military use.

'I don't want a whizz-bang up me Khyber.
I don't want me bollocks shot away.
I'd rather be in England. Merry, Merry England.
And fornicate me bleedin' life away'

British Army marching song

After the unprecedented horrors of Verdun and The Somme, both sides were reeling in shock by the time 1917 came around. Deep in winter, deeper in despair, neither side thought that they could withstand another year like the previous one. Morale was plunging in the trenches as well as at home, whether home be London, Paris or Berlin. German civilians endured unprecedented deprivation and hunger to help feed the war effort. They bitterly referred to the winter of 1916-17 as 'The Turnip Winter'.

But 1917 was to be a peculiar and in many ways decisive year. America would enter the war on the Allied side but would take a long time to mobilise and reach the battlefields of Europe. Grand imperial Russia would convulse and collapse in revolution, freeing up a huge German reserve army – but that too would take time. Siam (Thailand) would declare war on Germany – but that wouldn't matter much. Things were going to change – but first the opposing armies would have to survive 1917. Haig was promoted to Field Marshal in January, but was hated by Lloyd George, who swore in secret that he would never allow that man the freedom to sacrifice so many lives again.

In February the Germans reintroduced their policy of total submarine warfare much to the fury of the Americans. Starving Britain to death might now be the only way to defeat it – and the Germans thought the gamble worth the risk. They stepped up their aerial attacks on British civilians too. On June 13th alone, 158 civilians were killed in air raids on London and a further 425 wounded. Britain would later retaliate by bombing Germany with aircraft based in France.

Charles Samuel Myers who first coined the term '**Shell Shock**'.

Australian Advanced Dressing Station near **Ypres**. The wounded soldier in the lower left of the photo has a dazed, thousand-yard stare - a frequent symptom of "**shell-shock**".

The Hindenburg Line at **Bullecourt**.

Map of German **Siegfriedstellung defences**.

SHELL SHOCK

By 1915, it had been well recognised that something odd was happening to significant numbers of soldiers, something that had never been seen before. German soldiers, French soldiers, British soldiers – they all fell prey to it alike. It manifested itself in a wide range of neurological and physical symptoms, so at first doctors thought they were treating a wide range of different conditions. Some soldiers had uncontrollable diarrhoea. Others had violent cramps or spasms. Some went blind or lost the use of limbs. Insomnia accompanied by terrifying flashbacks tormented them. Others went insane, or turned their rifles on themselves.

At first the British army – and indeed the medical establishment - were sceptical about what they were seeing. Many officers thought the men were just acting up – and none too few were shot at dawn as a consequence. It was only when experienced men of the officer class started to come down with the same affliction that they changed their minds. The doctors thought they were seeing the outbreak of an odd new disease. Only slowly did it dawn on them what they were really being confronted with.

In 1915, a medical officer named Charles Myers first coined the term 'Shell Shock' in The Lancet. He thought that the condition was a physical injury to the nervous system brought about by proximity to heavy shelling. However, Myers quickly became dissatisfied by his own explanation. This was an outbreak of mental illness on an unheard of scale, caused by the sheer horror of the war and the need to force good men to do terrible things. It could be any one of thousand terrible things that had driven a man to breaking point and beyond. Some had bayoneted a man and stared into his eyes as he died. Others had been buried alive in mud and had to dig their way out of their own graves. Some had seen their best friends reduced to offal. The horror had simply broken them.

It's believed that over 80,000 British soldiers suffered from shell shock over the course of the war. Of those four fiths were never able to return to active service.

RETREAT TO THE HINDENBURG LINE

On the Western Front, the Germans had fought a largely defensive strategy since the failure of the Schlieffen Plan in 1914. Experience had taught them that whoever went 'over the top' would usually come off worst and that immediate counter-attacks to retake lost land were preferable to having to launch a later offensive against a well prepared and dug in enemy.

Hindenburg was a classical German defensive thinker. One of his first decisions after replacing Falkenhayn had been to construct the Siegfriedstellung – or what became known as The Hindenburg Line. Germany had suffered serious, almost grievous, losses at Verdun and on The Somme in 1916 and had realised it could not take another year of such losses. Now the response was to dig in deep and hard and just hold on. In 1917, the Germans anticipated, they would fight the Abwehrschlacht – the defensive battle.

The Hindenburg Line, based in the Noyes Salient and stretching from Arras to Chemin des Dames was just one of five massive defensive works. It stretched for over 100 miles and was constructed in just five months by a combined labour force of German civilians and Russian slave workers. A network of deep trenches were combined with steel-reinforced concrete blockhouses and then protected by barbed wire entanglements 60 feet wide. Defending these central areas were outlying positions and specially designed 'killing grounds' into which artillery and machine gun fire could be concentrated on advancing troops.

The debate about whether or not the German Army should retreat to these better prepared and stronger positions began almost as soon as construction got underway in September 1916. At first the idea seemed politically unacceptable. The German people might see it as an admission that the war wasn't going Germany's way. Troops might be demoralized to leave the old lines they had shed so much blood to defend and the Allies might even be encouraged by the sight of Germans turning their backs.

By March 1917, however, opinion changed and it was seen that 'relocating' to the Hindenburg Line was very much the right thing to do. The Germans launched Operation Alberich,

Surrey Yeomanry passing through the ruined village of Caulaincourt as the Germans Retreat to the Hindenburg Line.

Arthur Zimmermann.

Painting depicting the sinking of the Lusitania by the German U-Boat U 20.

with their forces on the Somme falling back to the Hindenburg Line. As they went, they carried out a systematic 'scorched earth' policy. They destroyed everything in their path –raising villages, burning crops, polluting wells and blowing up bridges. Livestock was shot. Everywhere they left booby-traps. The idea was that the Allies would find nothing they could use in the devastated landscape – and any advance would be slowed by obstacles and hidden bombs.

Now they sat, encased in concrete, behind their 'defence in depth' and killing grounds, guns ready. Just waiting for the next big Allied push...

AMERICA ENTERS THE WAR

America at the beginning of the 20th century was a very long way from Europe. It may have taken in Europe's poor and its huddled masses but it was keen to forge a strong new destiny of its own. It actively pursued an isolationist policy and, when war broke out in 1914, it was all too keen to stay out of the mess and remain neutral. Anti-war sentiment was strong in America, where press accounts of the slaughter in the trenches terrified and chilled American families. A strong religious lobby strove vigorously to denounce war as immoral and a sin, and to keep America as far away from it as possible. There was equally strong anti-British sentiment, particularly from German and Irish immigrants.

Throughout the early years of the war, America sought to profit from the situation by trading with both sides, but a British blockade of German ports saw its sales to the Central European powers collapse while sales to the Allies tripled. Now the Allies were a hugely important trading partner – until German submarines started sinking the merchant ships plying their trade in the Atlantic.

President Woodrow Wilson was caught up in a quandary. He came from a religious family and instinctively disliked war. He saw the complexity of the reasons that had taken Europe to war, and that there was not necessarily a 'good side' to be aided. Moreover he had been re-elected in 1916, largely because of the slogan, 'he kept us out of the war'. He had even tried – vainly – to spark peace talks between the warring

powers. Wilson did not want war. But war was what he was going to get.

On 1st February, Germany announced the resumption of unrestricted submarine warfare. Two days later, America formally severed all diplomatic ties with the Germans. The attacks on Atlantic shipping had always been a cause of tension between the two nations. The horrors of the sinking of the Lusitania in 1915 and the loss of many merchant ships since had brought matters to the boil.

But stranger things were happening behind the scenes. Anticipating that America would finally go to war with Germany over the resumption of submarine attacks, the Foreign Secretary of the German Empire, Arthur Zimmerman , sent a telegram to the German ambassador in Mexico on 16th January. It instructed him to try and get Mexico to declare war on America. In return, they would get financial aid as well as New Mexico, Texas, Utah, Nevada, California and Arizona after a German victory. The telegram was intercepted by British Intelligence. They knew what they had was dynamite – but there was a problem. If they told America about the content of the telegram, the Germans would know the British had broken their code. (The Mexicans, for their part, thought it was all a bit silly as the Americans would certainly crush them in any war).

On 19th February, the British disclosed the Zimmerman Telegram to the American ambassador in London. He was incredulous. At first he thought it had to be a forgery – but when shown proof of its authenticity he was outraged. By an elaborate subterfuge, they also managed to convince the Germans that they had a traitor in their Mexican embassy rather than that their code had been compromised. The telegram was openly published in the press on 1st March. Public opinion was heavily swayed in favour of action against the Germans, but the German and Irish lobbies still fought hard, desperately claiming the Zimmerman Telegram was a cynical hoax dreamed up by Britain. When, on 3rd March, Zimmerman went on record with the US press and said, 'I cannot deny it. It is true', the pro-German lobby collapsed.

The Zimmermann Telegram made one further provocative claim. It promised 'the ruthless employment of our submarines' – one more threat guaranteed to make American blood boil.

Meanwhile, President Wilson sought permission of congress to arm all merican merchant ships on

Uncle Sam's pointing finger to recruit soldiers for the American Army.

I WANT YOU for THE NAVY

PROMOTION FOR ANY ONE ENLISTING
APPLY ANY RECRUITING STATION
OR POSTMASTER

"WAKE UP, AMERICA!" boy scouts charge with flags flying during the great parade up Fifth avenue, days after the U.S. declared war on Germany on **April 6.**

Two American soldiers run past the remains of two German soldiers toward a bunker.

26th February. When they refused, he did it anyway under Executive Order. By 20th March Wilson had the unanimous support of his War Cabinet to declare war on Germany. He went before Congress to deliver his war address on 2nd April. He was, he said, appealing for a '*war to end all wars*' and to '*make the world safe for democracy*'. War was formally declared on 6th April 1917.

By early June, General John J. Pershing, Commander-in-Chief of the American Expeditionary Force (AEF), was in Europe, talking with the Allied high command. By 2nd July he had requested an army of a million men be despatched from America to fight on the Western Front. Just over a week later he revised that figure up to three million. By this time an advanced force of 14,000 were already in France. They would first take up position in the trenches near Nancy at the end of October 1917 – but it would be a long wait for the rest of the US troops to arrive. America had only a relatively small standing army (190,000 men) and Pershing was insistent that no new American soldiers would be sent overseas until they had been properly trained. Weapons were equally scarce and the first combat forces had to acquire British and French artillery, aircraft and tanks, which required further training.

By the end of 1917, four American divisions were finally ready for combat, assembled near Verdun and fastening bayonets. **It was a start.**

THE GRAND SPRING OFFENSIVE

From the moment he gained command of the French armies, Nivelle set about pushing for a grand Spring offensive, with French and British troops working together to smash and then occupy the German trenches on the Aisne River. He promised total victory and an effective end to the war – in just 48 hours. All he would need would be 1.2 million men and 7,000 artillery pieces to bring to bear.

Both French politicians and senior commanders had severe misgivings about the chances of Nivelle's grand offensive working. Some looked back at the appalling carnage on the Somme just the year before and anticipated a bloody repeat. The French War Minister resigned in alarm over the

plan – but Nivelle was not to be dissuaded. When Douglas Haig added his voice to the opposition, Nivelle shrugged and suggested he be replaced.

ARRAS AND VIMY RIDGE

To support Nivelle's grand offensive, the BEF were charged with carrying out diversionary attacks to both confuse the enemy and draw off precious troops from the main assault. Launched a week before Nivelle's attack, the offensive against the city of Arras utilised British troops as well as a combination of Newfoundland, Canadian, Australian and New Zealander units. The front to be attacked would range from Vimy Ridge in the north to Boullecourt in the south.

Before the assault, engineers – mostly New Zealanders - dug out 15 miles of tunnels both behind their lines and stretching across No Man's Land to the German defences. They also made full use of the existing sewer systems, natural caves and underground quarries that already peppered the area. They built secret tunnels for troop movements, kitchens and a 700 bed hospital. They wired everything up to be illuminated by electric light and even laid down an underground railway. It was a magnificent feat, capable of housing some 24,000 soldiers if required. They also tunnelled towards the enemy lines to lay down huge mines that would be exploded at the start of the battle as well as assault tunnels which could disgorge Allied troops just yards from the enemy trenches. In return, German sappers were utilised to dig their own tunnels, trying to intercept the Allied ones. When miners broke through to an enemy tunnel, there were often fierce hand-to-hand battles underground.

The British fought hard to gain and maintain air superiority in the skies over Arras for reconnaissance purposes. Unfortunately for them, Baron von Richthofen's infamous 'Flying Circus' had been assigned to the area by March 1917 and Allied losses were steep. In just five days, the Royal Flying Corps would lose 75 aircraft and the average life expectancy of an RFC pilot was measured at just 18 flying hours. As the offensive developed however, the RFC managed to push the odds back in their favour, by sheer weight of numbers and

Another Notch Chateau Thierry

U.S. Marines

"Another notch. Chateau Thierry. U.S. Marines". American World War I poster.
ABOVE: United States recruiting poster for women to enlist in the Navy.

Trench cookers of the **191st Siege Battery**, **Royal Garrison Artillery**, near the village of **Wancourt**.

Sappers of the Royal Engineers fix scaling ladders in front line trenches during **The Battle of Arras**.

The Infamous **"Flying Circus"**.

by bombing enemy airfields and catching their rivals on the ground.

The artillery barrage began on 20th March and expended over 2½ million shells. Gas was widely used, as well as a new kind of HE shell that tore barbed wire apart. Larger than the artillery bombardment on the Somme, it effectively dissolved the German's front line trenches. British and Dominion forces commenced their attack in the early hours of 9th April, in the face of a totally unexpected snowstorm.

The Canadians assaulted Vimy Ridge, which the Germans had spent two years fortifying. The ridge was a natural defensive position that rose to 500 feet and was considered impregnable. At dawn on 9th April, four Canadian divisions went 'over the top' and stormed the ridge. The odds were considered against them – but this was the most rehearsed assault in military history, meticulously planned by Lt. General Julian Byng and Major-General Arthur Currie. Troops were properly briefed in advance. They all knew the plan of battle and each carried his own map of the battleground. If their officers were killed they would therefore still know what to do. Every soldier too had rehearsed 'The Vimy Glide', advancing at just the right speed to keep behind the protective rolling barrage. They took their objective – the crest of Vimy Ridge - by 1pm on the first day of the assault.

British forces concentrated on objectives along the Scarpe River. They received heavy casualties in the first few days but took most of their objectives and advanced around 3 miles. Back at headquarters, General Ludendorff abandoned his birthday party and confessed to being 'deeply depressed' by the state of affairs. He took immediate steps to shore up the German defences which he thought had been badly mismanaged. German reinforcements were rushed into place. The Allies pressed on only to be met with stiff resistance and the area became nothing more than a grim battle of attrition. But by 16th April it was becoming obvious that something was going very badly wrong with the grand Nivelle Offensive and all their efforts might be in vain.

Australian and British forces combined around Bullecourt, but their initial offensive failed to break the German lines. Tank support proved ineffective and the Australians suffered their worst losses yet on the Western Front. It took until 3rd May for the Allies to be in a position to launch a second assault. A number of minor objectives were captured with fierce fighting, but losses were heavy. The Australians took to calling Bullecourt 'The Blood Tub'.

With the failure of the Nivelle Offensive, the situation round Arras settled into an uncomfortable stalemate.

Although this was a victory for the British and Dominion forces, their actions ultimately mattered little because they were merely intended as a diversion. Looking back at the battle Ludendorff himself confessed he was completely baffled by what the Allies objectives could have been. As of 16th May, British and Dominion forces had suffered around 160.000 casualties in the offensive and had gained nothing of any true strategic value. German losses were probably around 20,000 less. 25 Victoria Crosses were awarded.

Ludendorff used the stalemate to consider the success or failure of his defensive tactics and sacked several of his field commanders, including General von Falkenhausen on whom he laid the main blame. Falkenhausen was sent in disgrace to be Governor-General of Belgium where, hurt and offended by his dismissal, he presided over some 170 executions of Belgian civilians before disappearing from history.

THE NIVELLE OFFENSIVE

'*Have confidence and courage!*' Nivelle told his troops. '*The German Army will run away! They only want to be off.*' His grand promises of a devastating, war-ending assault lasting just 48 hours appeared in all the French newspapers and were the talk of Paris. Finally the war would be over. Morale amongst civilian and soldiers alike rose to new heights. Everyone was excited.

After three delays, the grand Nivelle Offensive on the Chemin des Dames Ridge was finally launched along a 40 mile front – and nothing went well from the very start. The Germans had captured the French battle plans a few days earlier and were now fully prepared for the assault. Nivelle knew his plans had been compromised – but refused to change or abandon them. He also refused to halt his plans even though he

Baron Captain Manfred von Richthofen.

German prisoners of war on the march to confinement areas behind Canadian lines.

French Schneider-tank.

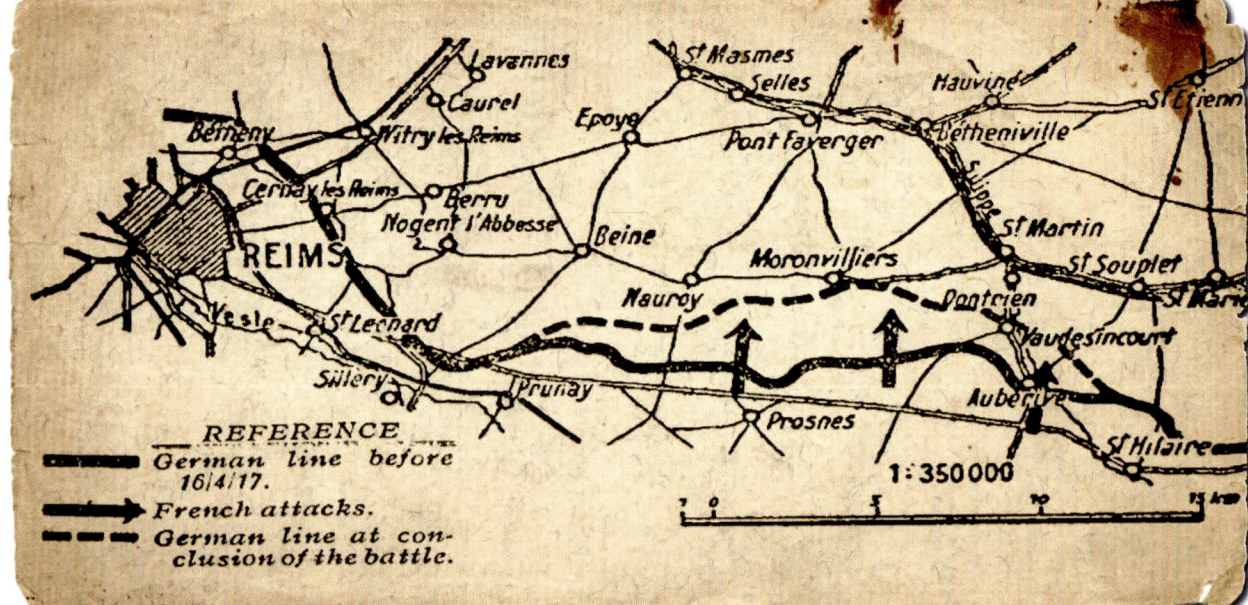

REFERENCE

German line before 16/4/17.

French attacks.

German line at conclusion of the battle.

1:350000

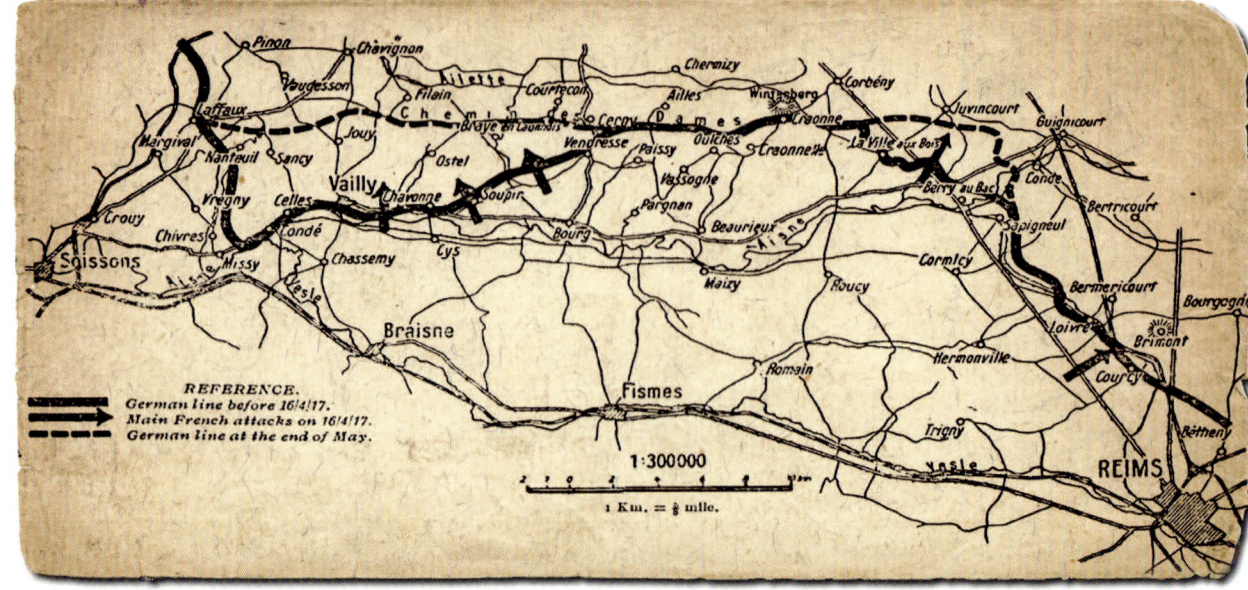

REFERENCE.

German line before 16/4/17.

Main French attacks on 16/4/17.

German line at the end of May.

1:300000

1 Km. = ⅝ mile.

had far fewer artillery pieces available than he had intended, with the result that the opening artillery barrage was far less effective than it could have been.

On the first day of the offensive, April 16th, the French suffered 40,000 casualties. Nivelle had estimated 10,000 over the entire duration of the offensive. The Germans for their part were utterly baffled by the French tactics, watching wave after wave of the finest French regiments being torn to pieces by relentless machine gun fire as they emerged struggling uphill through driving rain and sleet in the early morning light. To make matters even worse, the very tactic that Nivelle had pioneered – the creeping barrage - was incorrectly used by French artillery, further weakening protection for the advancing troops. One French officer taking part in the assault noted, *'The battle began at six. By seven it had been lost'.*

Subsequent days fared little better – but Nivelle refused to admit he was wrong and call off the attacks. Instead as his grand offensive progressively stalled and failed, Nivelle became increasingly anxious and depressed and started to lose control of the situation. He felt the full weight of the French government's scrutiny upon him and they in turn began to make decisions for him. He had promised them everything – and delivered next to nothing. Now everything was crumbling. He was running short of artillery shells and – such was the sheer scale of his casualties - the French medical services were no longer able to cope with the evacuation of the wounded. Furthermore, most of the Schneider tanks deployed by Nivelle had been destroyed on the battlefield by effective German artillery fire – almost 150 of them on the very first day of battle.

The Nivelle Offensive was finally abandoned on 9th May after an estimated 187,000 French casualties and a further 150,000 British and Commonwealth losses. Nivelle was unceremoniously replaced by Petain as French Commander-in-Chief just six days later. He was then promoted sideways to head up French regiments in North Africa where he could do no more harm.

French gains on the **Aisne, April-May 1917.**
ABOVE: French gains in **Champagne, April-May 1917.**

German pioneers and soldiers at work on a supply route of the **Chemin des Dames.**

Execution at **Verdun** at the time of the mutinies.

Australian infantry of the **45th Battalion, Australian 4th Division** wearing Small Box Respirators at **Garter Point** near **Zonnebeke, Ypres sector.**

THE FRENCH MUTINIES

'Everyone has really had enough.'

French soldier, 74th Infantry Regiment

Nivelle had raised the hopes of a nation and its army sky-high. The war was about to be won. Now, as his vaunted offensive fell apart in abject failure, morale plunged – and was replaced by deep and bitter anger.

As it dawned on the French troops taking part in the Nivelle Offensive that their grand assault was failing, the first traces of outright mutiny began to stir in their ranks. Some soldiers made plaintiff bleating noises directly into the faces of their superior officers, indicating that they were nothing but 'lambs to the slaughter'. The French 2nd Colonial Division went further, getting drunk and then turning up for battle without their rifles.

Already shaken by the sheer carnage at Verdun, in which virtually every division in the French Army had participated, the Nivelle Offensive had proved the final straw. Over 1,000,000 French soldiers had been killed since the war began. And for what?

By June, the mutiny had spread to some 68 French divisions. 20,000 soldiers simply deserted. Officers were rarely if ever attacked. Their men simply refused to return from the rear to their trenches. One unit took to wearing flowers in the lapels of their trenchcoats, and told their officers exactly where they stood – *'You have nothing to fear. We are prepared to man the trenches, we will do our duty and the Germans will not get through. But we will not take part in attacks which result in nothing but useless casualties .'* Others sang the communist anthem, 'The Internationale'.The French Army had become an ineffective fighting force.

The French had seen mutinies earlier in the war – and had resorted to a version of the Roman Legion tactic of 'decimation'. A number of men from a mutinous unit would be chosen at random by lottery and shot – to set an example to the survivors. When (untrue) rumours started to spread that this policy would be used against them now, it only stiffened the resolve of the mutineers and further incited them to rebellion.

Petain took a very different approach, perhaps because of his sympathy for the troops and perhaps because it was impractical to start shooting groups of men from half the entire French Army. Instead, he largely acquiesced to the mutineers' demands.

Petain increased soldiers' leave, pay and rations (the soldiers had taken to calling their food 'monkey meat'). At the same time, executions for mutiny were greatly scaled back. 554 soldiers were sentenced to death - but only 49 were ever brought before the firing squad. Most important of all in ending the mutinies, Petain strongly suggested that the French would launch no more mass offensives and would concentrate only on defensive actions. This suited Petain well, as he had never been enthusiastic about the tactics of mass infantry offensives. It would be left to the British to take the offensive in future – at least until the Americans arrived.

By 17th June, the mutiny was considered to be over. Somehow the French authorities had managed to keep the whole affair hidden from the Germans – and even their own British Allies.

THE FLANDERS OFFENSIVE

'...I died in hell (They called it Passchendaele)'

Siegfried Sassoon.

In June 1917, Haig finally got what he wanted for the past two years – permission to launch a grand offensive against the enemy in Flanders. The official objective was finally to break out of the Ypres Salient and start recapturing Belgian ports used by U-boat raiders. Unofficially, there was also a desperate need to help take the pressure off the French forces which had been seriously damaged by Nivelle's Offensive and the mutinies which followed. Haig – with his usual optimism - believed that there was a good chance the Germans here were near to collapse and might indeed do so if pressed.

Preparations for the offensive had been underway since the previous year, with teams of British engineers secretly tunnelling under the German fortifications at the Wytschaete Ridge at Messines south of Ypres. German field officers had detected traces of the mining, but their superiors had failed to act. Now, on 7th June, the Battle of Messines commenced with

General Sir Herbert Plumer on Front cover of Le Pays de France.

An 18 pounder gun being hauled through the mud at **Broodseinde Ridge.**

Wounded at side of the road. **Battle of Menin Road.**

Destroyed German trench, dead German soldiers lie amidst the rubble on **Messines Ridge.**

Artillery barrage map from Battle of Menin Road during the Third Battle of Ypres.

the detonation of 19 truly colossal explosive charges under German lines. 10,000 German soldiers were thought to have been blown to pieces in the detonations and the explosions were heard as far away as Paris and London. Advancing British and Dominion infantry from the 2nd Army under the command of General Herbert Plumer quickly secured and then held the strategically vital ridge over the next week of fighting. It was a striking victory – but marred by severe casualties caused to the II Anzacs by friendly fire from Allied artillery.

Delighted by his success at Messines, Haig quickly planned another offensive, this time to strike north east of Ypres. British troops from the 5th and the 2nd Armies, supported by elements of the French 1st Army, would break out of the Ypres Salient, assault the German defensive lines and seize Passchendaele Ridge. From here they would be perfectly positioned to sweep north again and free the ports of Ostend and Zeebrugge, which was home to U-boat pens, as well as the railway hub at Roulers. Haig launched his assault with a full ten day artillery barrage, with 3,000 big guns pumping an incredible 4 ¼ million artillery shells down onto German 4th Army positions. As at the Somme, the artillery barrage failed to adequately crack German heavy fortifications. Instead its principle effect was to tell the Germans just where the Allied assault was to be launched.

At 3.50 am on 31st July, the Allies went 'over the top' along an eleven mile wide front, supported by a creeping barrage. Their timing could not have been worse. It began to rain furiously just a few hours after the assault started, creating chaos. The battlefield, churned and pitted by the bombardment, proved slow and slippery to traverse. Any tanks deployed soon broke down or became stuck fast. The Germans were able to fend off the slow-moving assault in most places along the front. To the north of the line, the Allies managed to gain some objectives but completely failed elsewhere.

And it continued to rain, and rain again all through the summer and into autumn – the worst rain recorded in 30 years -as the Allies struggled to make any more significant progress. A war correspondent for the Daily Mail described the scene on 2nd August in one of his despatches from the front:

'Floods of rain and a blanket of mist have doused and cloaked the whole of the Flanders plain. The newest shell-holes, already half-filled with soakage, are now flooded to the brim. The rain has so fouled this low, stoneless ground, spoiled of all natural drainage by shell-fire... that men could scarcely walk in full equipment, much less dig. Every man was soaked through and was standing or sleeping in a marsh. It was

a work of energy to keep a rifle in a state fit to use.'

The field of battle soon became one vast treacherous quagmire of sucking mud, pitted with deep shell craters filled with rain and drainage water. Numerous men sank in them and were drowned or choked to death, never to be found again. Half submerged corpses were used as stepping stones until they too were pressed underground and disappeared from sight. Some shell holes were so deep they could – and did – trap and drown donkeys and horses. Eyewitnesses described shells hitting the mud and hurling hidden bodies high into the air, disintegrating as they went. The word 'hell' was used frequently by both sides, and the fields of sodden filth produced some of the most memorable and terrible images of the entire war. Morale on both sides began to crack.

In the Daily Express for 17th August, Percival Phillips gave a vivid account of the attack on Langemarck:

'I talked today with a number of wounded men engaged in the fighting in Langemarck and beyond, and they are unanimous in declaring that the enemy infantry made a very poor show wherever they were deprived of their supporting machine guns and forced to choose between meeting a bayonet charge and flight. The mud was our men's greatest grievance. It clung to their legs at every step. Frequently they had to pause to pull their comrades from the treacherous mire - figures embedded to the waist, some of them trying to fire their rifles at a spitting machine gun and yet, despite these almost incredible difficulties, they saved each other and fought the Hun through the floods to Langemarck.'

A British officer, Edward Vaughan, noted:

'The cries of the wounded had much diminished now and as we staggered down the road, the reason was only too apparent, for the water was right over the tops of the shell-holes.'

When the weather finally improved in mid-September that year, Haig pressed on with renewed vigour, achieving victories at Menin Road Ridge, Polygon Wood and finally Broodseinde on the 4th October. Little more was achieved in October, as the driving rains returned.

British and Canadian troops finally took the village of Passchendaele on 6th November, after earlier bloody assaults by the New Zealanders and Australians. What was intended as a swift campaign had in reality taken over three months and cost 325,000 Allied dead and wounded – for the gain of a little over five miles. German casualties were reckoned to be in the region of 260,000. Many were lost forever beneath the sucking mud. There are 35,000 names of soldiers who have no known grave on the Tyne Cot Memorial at Passchendaele alone.

The slaughter of Canadians at Passchendaele caused the

British soldiers in trenches with tank in background.

Kaiser Wilhelm II & Emperor Crown Prince Rupprecht of Bavaria on the way to visit troops at **The Battle Of Cambria.**

A British **Mark IV** tank at Wailly. This shows how it would appear to occupants of the German trenches during the Battle of Cambrai.

furious Canadian Prime Minister to complain to Lloyd George. *'The gain was not worth the candle,'* he said. *'The result was not worth the loss.'* The Prime Minister of New Zealand also added his voice to the protest, saying, *'The New Zealanders were asked to do the impossible and were shot down like rabbits'.*

THE BATTLE OF CAMBRAI

The British launched a mass tank assault at Cambrai on 20th November. Over 450 Mark IV tanks along a 10,000 yard front rolled into battle against the German 2nd Army defending part of the Hindenburg Line, supporting elements of the British 3rd Army. It commenced with a fast thousand gun barrage. The tanks succeeded in tearing paths through the deep barbed wire entanglements for the infantry to follow but their armour quickly proved no match for determined artillery and even infantry action. 65 were destroyed – 16 by a single German battery. Over 70 broke down and 43 got stuck in ditches or trench works. On the first day, the Hindenburg Line was penetrated to a depth of 5 miles, but further advances towards Cambrai were stopped when a tank captured a vital canal bridge – and then accidentally demolished it under its own weight while trying to cross. Over 8,000 German prisoners were taken and 100 German big guns captured. The news was greeted by wild celebration in Britain, where church bells were rung throughout the land for the first time since the outbreak of war. *'Haig Through the Hindenburg Line!'* announced the Daily Mail on 23rd November.

Their celebrations were sadly premature. British commanders were so astonished by their own success that they failed to build on it. They stalled, often just short of their objectives, and began to prepare rudimentary defences. Over the next few days, the Germans reorganised and launched a succession of determined counter-attacks. These often utilised new infiltration techniques spearheaded by elite storm troopers and caused alarm, surprise and confusion in the hastily arranged British defences. They finally succeeded in driving the British back to their starting point by 7th December and even gaining fresh ground in a few places. Each side lost between 40,000-50,000 men. The loss of ground after such a spectacular initial breakthrough prompted a court of enquiry.

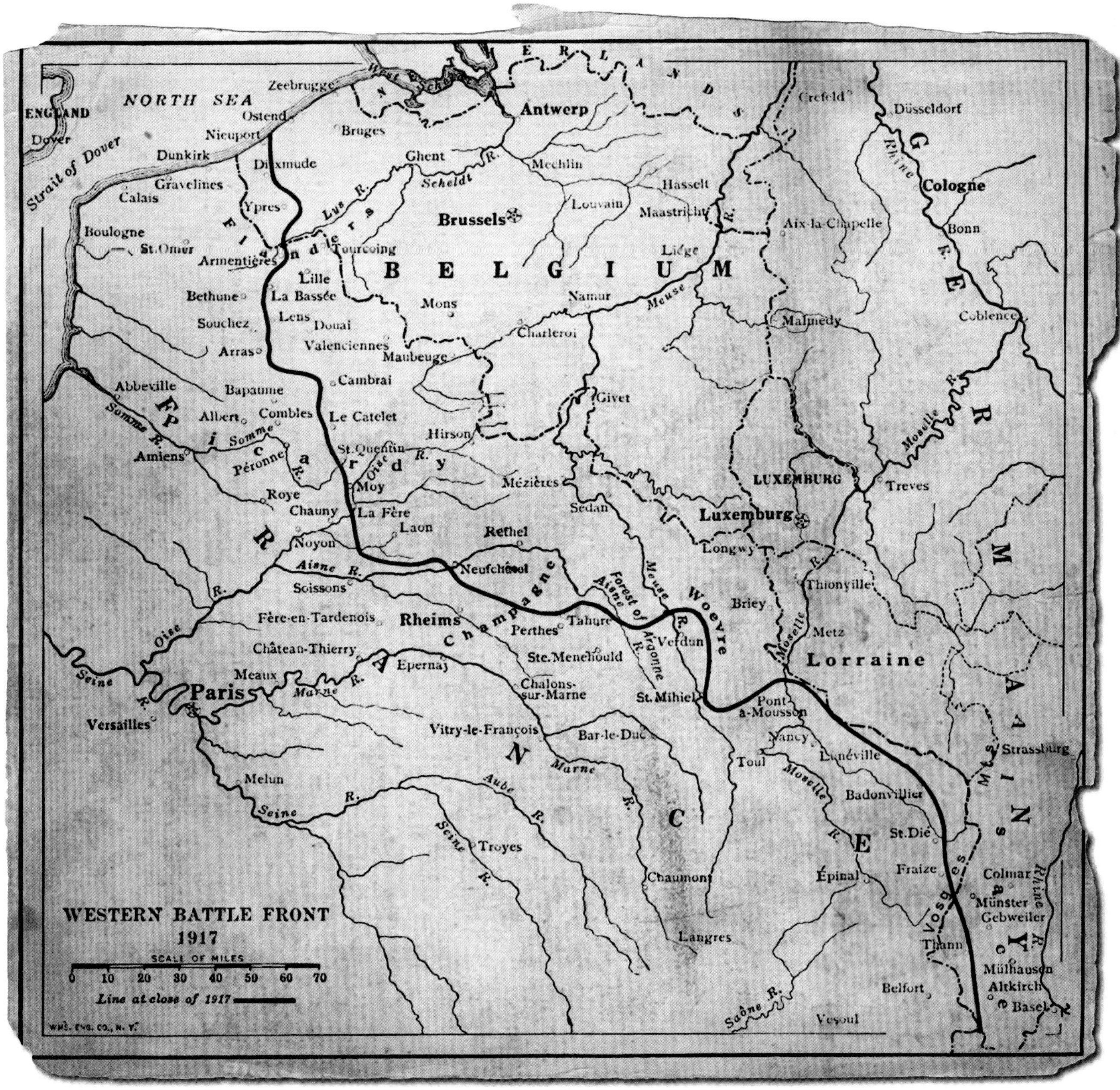

The Western Front line in 1917.

WESTERN BATTLE FRONT 1917

SCALE OF MILES

0   10   20   30   40   50   60   70

Line at close of 1917 ——————

German soldiers in fighting position with gas masks and machine gun at the front line during a gas attack in 1917.

America joins the war.

Operations on the Ancre, British troops in a captured German trench, Serre.

Battle of Cambrai. Men of the 11th Leicester Regiment (6th Division) with machine guns in captured 2nd line trench.

Painting of the Battle of Vimy Ridge by Richard Jack.

Tanks in a field station.

1918

'We must strike at the earliest moment before the Americans can throw strong forces into the scale. We must beat the British.'

Ludendorff

By the start of 1918, it was becoming increasingly clear that this would be the decisive year of the war. Both sides now possessed a fresh advantage to break the stalemate and whoever managed to take full advantage of it – correctly and first – would win. November 1917 had seen the collapse of war on the Eastern Front as Russia fell to the communists, and forty four German divisions were freed up to fight on the Western Front. On the Allied side, America had now entered the war and was frantically building new armies and new ships to take them to Europe.

If the two fresh forces met at exactly the same time there might be the mother of all bloodbaths and then the mother of all stalemates – but if one side could press home the advantage first, they could win. Now Germany, who had largely fought a cautious and defensive war until this point, decided to gamble everything on one last vast offensive...

They named it Kaiserschlacht – the Kaiser's Battle.

A 60-pounder Gun recoils firing from an open position near **La Boiselle**. at the **Battle of Bapaume**.

German tank drives through the streets of **Roye**.

French Marshal Ferdinand Foch.

OPERATION MICHAEL

The first phase of the grand offensive was named after Michael, Germany's patron saint.

The Allies knew they were coming, but there was little they could do except wait. Haig had begged the politicians for 600,000 more men. They had sent him just 100,000, fearful that he might use them all up in one huge and bloody offensive. And the Americans weren't nearly ready yet.

Operation Michael began on 21st March, when 6,600 German big guns unleashed a barrage along a 60 mile front on the Somme. Over 1,000,000 shells fell on Allied positions in just five hours – 3,000 shells a minute and the most intense bombardment of the war to date. One in four was a gas shell. Then Minister of Munitions Winston Churchill was caught up in the bombardment as he inspected troops and later wrote:

'...there rose in less than one minute the most tremendous cannonade I shall ever hear...the enormous explosions of the shells upon our trenches seemed almost to touch each other, with hardly an interval in space or time...The weight and intensity of the bombardment surpassed anything which anyone had ever known before.'

62 Divisions went over the top to attack 26 divisions of the British 3rd and 5th Armies. The aim was to drive a thick wedge between the French and British armies on the Somme, destroy vital railway supply lines and then role up and annihilate the British entirely.

They used elite storm troopers, aided by thick fog and swirling poison gas, to sweep around British strongpoints and create holes where the defences were weakest. They moved rapidly, sowing confusion, attacking command posts and supply dumps, using flame throwers to create terror and allowing the forces that followed them to neutralise the more secure Allied positions as and when they could.

The British defensive lines were already weak. They lay in a sector previously occupied by the French and the British had only just moved into the area to find it woefully maintained. There had been little if any time to improve the defences before the Germans struck. The British 5th Army suffered a shattering defeat that left it almost ineffective as a fighting unit. Within just two days it was in full retreat and in just two weeks the Germans managed to recapture every scrap of land they had lost at the Somme in 1916.

A delighted Kaiser declared 24th March to be a national holiday and many on the German Home Front started to believe that victory was in sight. The French meanwhile hastily promoted a more aggressive commander, Marshal Ferdinand Foch, over Petain who was expressing a strong opinion that the Allies *'should wait for the tanks and the Americans'*. Foch would now act as Allied Supreme Commander.

The British 3rd Army however held – and held well. It prevented the advancing Germans from capturing their main objectives of Arras and Amiens. The assault on the latter was stopped dead by the British 51st Division, making full use of tanks to blast mass German infantry as they advanced over flat open fields towards the town. German casualties were appalling.

The Allies lost some 255,000 troops compared to a German casualty figure of 239,000. However, among the German dead and wounded were a huge number of their elite storm troops – men who could neither be spared nor easily replaced.

OPERATION GEORGETTE

The second phase of the great German Spring Offensive began on 9th April, as 46 divisions of the German 6th Army surged forward against the beleaguered British and Portuguese lines protecting Ypres. At the first, the Allies were hurled backwards by the sheer force of the assault, losing the strategic – and hard won – Passchendaele Ridge and stumbling back almost to the outskirts of Ypres itself. It was feared that the Germans might be able to seize the Channel Ports in under a week. On 11th April, Haig ordered:

'With our backs to the wall and believing in the justice of our cause, each one of us must fight on to the end.'

The defenders were only saved from being overrun, literally in the nick of time, by the arrival of Australian, French and other British reinforcements, who managed to battle the Germans to a bloody standstill by 29th April. Apart from reinforcements, another decisive factor was Allied air superiority which was beginning to play an ever-more important part in the conflict. Allied aircraft found the

British **55th (West Lancashire) Division** troops blinded by gas await treatment at an Advanced Dressing Station near **Bethune** during the **Battle of Estaires**.

German stormtrooper with his **Bergmann MP18.1** and a **Parabellum P08**.

Erich Von Ludendorff.

The bodies of dead French soldiers lie shallow trench.

massed German formations which followed their storm troopers into action easy targets and they were relentlessly strafed or bombed. Later reports estimated that a full half of all German casualties during Operation Georgette resulted from air attacks. Around 110,000 men had been killed or wounded on each side.

THE BLUCHER YORCK OFFENSIVE

The final wave of Ludendorff's grand Spring Offensive began on 27th May, as 41 German divisions were hurled against the French 6th Army around the Chemin des Dames Ridge in Central France. Accompanying the French were six exhausted British divisions who were officially 'resting'. The aim was to stop the 6th being used to reinforce Allied positions on the Somme or at Ypres. Instead, it succeeded beyond Ludendorff's wildest dreams. After a lethal 4,500 gun artillery barrage and a devastatingly effective assault led by storm troopers, the French 6th crumbled and effectively fell apart all along a 25 mile front east of the Aisne River. The Germans advanced almost 10 miles in a single day – the greatest progress any side had made on the Western Front since the start of 1915.

Ludendorff decided to gamble everything – and head for Paris. In just two days, the Germans had crossed the Aisne in great numbers, and soon arrived on the Marne and found themselves within just 37 miles of the French capital. Once more, Parisians began to flee and the French government looked towards finding temporary safety in Bordeaux.

Fully aware of the threat, the Allies threw 27 divisions of French and American soldiers against the advancing Germans. The line held. At Belleau Wood over three weeks in June the U.S. 2nd Infantry Division held the Germans firmly at bay and had 5,000 men killed in action in the process - but they probably saved Paris.

THE GNEISENAU OFFENSIVE

In a desperate hurry to capitalise on his unexpected proximity to Paris, Ludendorff hastily cobbled together a further plan of attack – the Gneisenau Offensive. Troops of his 18th Army struck south-west towards Paris on 9th June.

At first the German divisions, despite their parlous state, looked like they would achieve one final, glorious victory. Placing 21 divisions in the field, Ludendorff saw his men advance no less than 9 miles – before they were stopped dead in their tracks by a determined and completely unexpected counter-attack by the French under General Charles 'The Butcher' Mangin, meeting the advancing Germans with 4 divisions, 150 tanks and full air support at Compiegne. The German offensive crumbled within just four days.

THE FAILURE OF KAISERSCHLACHT

What had started as a brilliant success for the Germans suddenly began to look like a dangerous failure. No one had learned the lessons of the failure of the Schlieffen Plan – and there were new problems to face. As Ludendorff surveyed the overall situation, he almost collapsed – and his subordinates began to fear he would either commit suicide or go insane. He had gambled Imperial Germany herself on this offensive, won magnificently and still lost.

Everywhere his troops were exhausted and could not press home the advantage. They had suffered enormous losses – including many irreplaceable elite troops – which had not been expected. The British in particular had adopted the German tactic of defence in depth and, wherever it had been properly applied, German losses were always ferocious. By June 1918, it was estimated that Kaiserschlacht had cost them a million soldiers.

The Germans had also experienced severe problems with supplying their forward troops. The storm troopers carried little supplies and had pushed forward so far that supply trains could not keep up with them. Many units were almost starving. In places, the Germans were forced to kill their own horses to have something to eat and, when advancing forces came across stocked shops in the high street of Armentieres, discipline broke down completely as they went on an orgy of looting. Wherever captured wine or rum was discovered, there was soon widespread drunkenness and stupor. Supply problems had been one of the major reasons for the failure of the Schlieffen Plan, but things were actually worse in 1918. Much of the landscape had been obliterated by years of warfare, churning up supply roads and interrupting rail routes.

Built for speed

and with light pack to match

P. B-
Belleau Wood
1918
A Marine

Sketch of Soldier with light pack "Built for speed" Signed Belleau Wood 1918 A Marine.

German infantry division crosses a conquered British position.

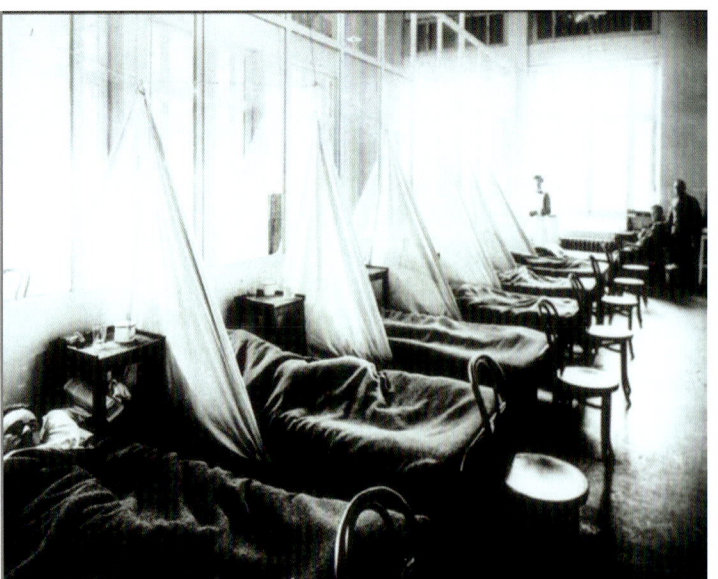

U.S. Army Camp Hospital No. 45, **Aix-Les-Bains,** during the **Influenza pandemic.**

French troopers under **General Gouraud,** amongst the ruins of a church near the **Marne,** driving back the Germans.

Most painful of all, the Germans themselves had employed a scorched earth tactic against the territories they moved through when they retreated to the Hindenburg Line in 1917. Expanded outwards again, they found themselves in a barren wilderness of their own making.

There were even rumours of German troops if not mutinying then at least showing a reluctance to participate in further attacks. And now the German Army, weakened by relentless combat and lack of food was starting to be hit by a mysterious new illness – one which would become known as Spanish Flu and would eventually kill 27,000,000 people around the world before vanishing as mysteriously as it began. In June 1918 alone, 500,000 German soldiers came down with the sickness.

But what of their undeniable territorial gains? Surely that had to count for something? As Ludendorff looked at his maps, he began to realise that his men had seized almost exclusively strategically useless territory. His army had captured next to none of its main targets and instead found itself in bulges or salients that were vulnerable to attack on three sides and so required huge resources to defend – resources Ludendorff couldn't spare.

Racked with sickness, short of ammunition, short of reinforcements, short of food and water, the German army was overstretched – and vulnerable.

THE SECOND BATTLE OF THE MARNE

More out of desperation than inspiration, the faltering Germans tried yet one more offensive. On 15th July 1918, 23 divisions of the German 1st and 3rd Armies attacked the French 4th and the American 42nd division to the east of Reims, while a further 17 German divisions of the German 7th and 9th attacked the French 6th to the west, hoping to split the French forces in two.

The Germans launched their offensive with a substantial artillery barrage. However, they had been tricked. The French had set up an elaborate system of dummy trenches and the Germans targeted these by mistake. Virtually unharmed by the bombardment in their real trench lines, the French and

WESTERN BATTLE FRONT
July 15, 1918

SCALE OF MILES

0   10 20   40   60   80

Battle Line, July 15, 1918

The Western Front line July 15 1918.

Heavy shells on trolleys in a Emplacement on the road **Amiens-Albert.**

Downed British Tank **Mark IV Amiens.**

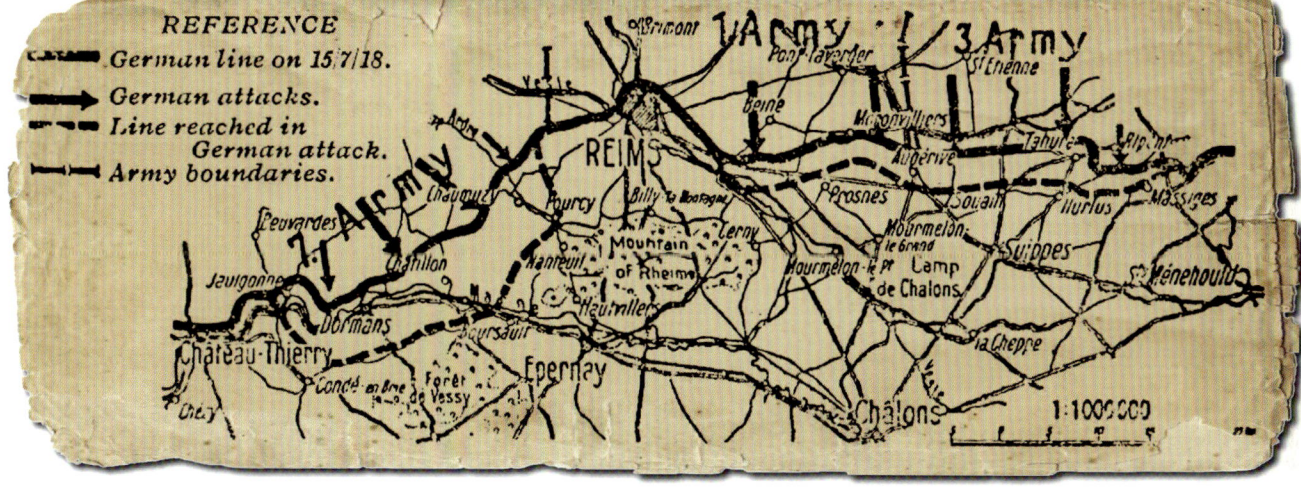

Americans were well prepared for them when they came, with artillery blasting bloody swathes out of the massed German infantry as they tried to advance over open ground. The attack to the east collapsed in just a couple of hours but the western assault succeeded in capturing the banks of the River Marne. German engineers rapidly built pontoon bridges as storm trooper units used dinghies to swarm across the river, all the while under fire from Allied units on the far bank and 225 French bombers dropping 40 tons of high explosives all along the river positions.

The Germans were over the vital river – but the Allied line of defence held them on 17th July, with British, American. Italian and French forces all in furious action. The next day, forces under the command of Foch launched a massive counter-attack. 22 French divisions, joined by 10 American divisions, struck against the Germans in their precarious positions with their backs to the Marne River. The infantry were supported by 400 new Renault FT tanks. The Germans were hurled back across the river in disarray the following day, having suffered 168,000 casualties in just four days. They were a spent force never to go the offensive again.

It was, in all respects, the beginning of the end.

The fighting along the Marne cost the Germans around 139,000 dead and wounded as well as 29,367 captured. Allied dead and wounded numbered 95,165 French, 16,552 British, and 12,000 Americans. The counterattack at the Marne was first in a series of Allied offensives that would ultimately end the war. Two days after the battle's end, British troops attacked at Amiens.

AMIENS

Having successfully held and pushed back the German forces on the Marne, the Allies had taken the measure of the enemy's abilities and found it lacking. It was time for the real 'big push'. Preparations were to be top secret. Each British soldier received a small notice in his paybook that said simply , 'Keep Your Mouth Shut'.

On 8th August, the British 4th Army with Australian and Canadian Corps under Sir Henry Rawlinson, supported by 580 tanks, assaulted German positions around Amiens on the Somme. It was the single greatest concentration of tanks in the entire war, combining small Whippet tanks that would probe

German defences with heavier vehicles to take on and shell the better fortified German positions. The aim was to secure railway lines around the town stretching between Mericourt and Hangest, and they were supported in the action by 8 divisions of the 1st French Army.

There was thick fog on the battlefield and no preliminary artillery bombardment – just a 700 gun creeping barrage as the Allies advanced. The six German divisions facing them were caught by surprise and effectively fell apart. The Allies advanced a full seven miles and forced a gap in the German lines 15 miles wide while overhead planes of the newly formed Royal Air Force dropped phosphorous bombs on the fleeing enemy. Even British cavalry units finally got in on the action, harassing the enemy rear. In just a few hours, the Allies scooped up over 16,000 prisoners. Such was the speed of the assault that a number of senior German officers were literally caught still having breakfast. Some defending German units failed to even fire a single shot in defence before they were overwhelmed. A major in the Australian Corps said:

'The Germans were surrendering everywhere. We knew it was going to be the end of the war.'

This was, said Ludendorff *'the black day of the German Army'.* Reports reached him of his field officers being abused by their own men as they tried to stop the headlong retreat.

German Map showing the retreat fighting on the **Somme** in **Bray-Proyar.**
ABOVE: Map of German attacks on the **Marne and Champagne, July 1918**.

Canadian troops along **Arras-Cambrai road** in September, 1918.

Lt. General Julian Byng.

German Vice Admiral Hipper and staff.

'You're just prolonging the war,' they moaned. Others jeered at their own reinforcements as they marched forward, calling them *'blacklegs'*.

The Allied advance was only stopped when Ludendorff rushed nine divisions in to hold the line – his last available reserves. However, he told the Kaiser that the war was now effectively lost and that the only reason to fight on was to gain a better bargaining position when the time came to surrender. The Kaiser reluctantly agreed with his assessment.

THE '100 DAY OFFENSIVE' BEGINS

'Tout le monde a la bataille!'
(Everyone in the fight!)
Allied rallying cry, 1918.

The Allied success at Amiens stunned everyone – Allied and German alike. It was proof that the German Army was falling apart as a fighting machine and now was the perfect time for the Allies to go on the offensive and not stop.

Fighting continued around Amiens after 8th August for several days. As usual, although effective in the initial assault, the Allied tank force had rapidly broken down after actually being used. Within four days of going 'over the top' of the 580 tanks that had started the assault, only six were in any fit state to carry on fighting. Allied infantry and cavalry had also advanced beyond the effective range of their supporting big guns and, without tank and artillery support, Allied units found the fighting slower and harder going. ommunications between the advanced forces

and the lines they had left were increasingly tenuous. Foch was keen to carry on but Haig convinced him that the best course of action was to halt the advance on 12th August, consolidate the victory and then launch a fresh attack against the enemy between Ancre and Scarpe, using Byng's 3rd Army.

On 20th August the French 10th Army went on the offensive and took the heights around the Aisne River, capturing 8,000 despondent German soldiers in the process. Byng's 3rd Army launched its offensive on 21st August, striking at Arras along a ten mile front. The 4th Army joined in along with French forces, commencing a German retreat that didn't stop until they reached the relative safety of their own Hindenburg Line.

ASSAULTING THE HINDENBURG LINE

By early September 1918, except for some precarious salients, the German Army had fallen back to its old March 1917 positions along the heavily fortified Hindenburg Line.

Foch decided to attack in three massive waves. British, French and Belgian forces would strike at Flanders with King Albert of Belgium as its figurehead leading the assault. Haig would take control in the centre, attacking the very heart of the Hindenburg Line between Cambrai and St. Quentin, while the French and Americans would strike in the south between Reims and Verdun.

The Americans launched their first-ever solo offensive on 12th September, with their 1st Army hitting a remaining German salient at the southernmost point of the Western Front at St. Mihiel close to Verdun. Resistance was chaotic and disorganised, as the Germans were in the process of falling back when attacked. In less than two days, backed by French tanks and 600 Allied aircraft, the 1st had taken 15,000 Germans prisoner.

On 26th September, the American 1st joined with the French 4th to drive the Germans from the area between the Meuse River and the Argonne Forest. Here the offensive fared much less well, with the Germans choosing to stand and fight hard from well prepared and fortified defences. In six weeks of brutal fighting, the Americans suffered over 75,000 casualties. Progress was measured in just yards, as relentless rain turned

Sailors from the battleship **"Prince Regent Luitpold"** with blackboard *"Soldiers warship Prince Regent Luitpold. Long live the Socialist Republic".*

Sailors in **Wilhelmshaven** demonstrate after the uprising in 1918.

US Wounded being treated by 110th Sanitary Train, 4th Ambulance Corps, 1st Division, in an old church, **Neuville, Meuse.**

the battlefield into a quagmire pitted with deep flooded shell holes.

On 27th September, Haig threw 40 Allied divisions including Canadians and the American II Corps against 57 German divisions. For once, the numbers were not in the attacker's favour and the Hindenburg Line's already formidable defences were bolstered here by a series of wide canals with steep banks, some 60 feet high. These canals became the centrepieces of the fighting, with the British 1st and 3rd assaulting the Canal du Nord at the Battle of Cambrai-St. Quentin and then the 4th storming the St. Quentin Canal two days later. Here, the 46th North Midlanders managed to seize a vital canal bridge at Riqueval to the south and hold it as Allied troops stormed over. The Hindenburg line was broken on the 3rd October 1918. Once through though, the Allies were met with stubborn resistance almost everywhere they advanced. The Germans formed a new defensive line near Cambrai. It was taken after a battle raging from 9th-10th October. Now the Germans fell back to another defensive line on the Selle River. This was breached on 17th October and fighting moved on mid-month to Le Cateau. Now the Germans fell back to the Sambre River, a new defensive line which was assaulted on 4th November. German forces then fell back towards Mons, which was captured by the Canadians on 11th November on the morning of the armistice itself.

The Allied assault in Flanders began on 28th September 1918, with what became known as the Fourth Battle of Ypres. Allied forces made rapid advances, seizing back all the territory the Germans had gained from Operation Georgette and extending their lines forward some ten miles in just three days. However, the offensive slowed as heavy rains once more turned the battlefields into quagmires. The offensive resumed on 14th October at the Battle of Courtrai and the Allies pressed on northwards, retaking Douai, Ostend and Lille on the 17th October and Zeebrugge and Bruges two days later. By the end of October, the offensive had advanced 50 miles and was poised on the Scheldt River.

THE KIEL MUTINY

At the end of October 1918, while the rest of Germany was contemplating complete surrender, the German Imperial Navy suddenly got a taste for battle. Having been cooped up in port for most of the war, Naval Supreme Commander Admiral Reinhardt Scheer and Admiral Franz von Hipper abruptly decided to go out with all guns blazing in one last all-out giant sea battle with the Royal Navy. Unfortunately for von Hipper, his enthusiasm was not shared by many of his ratings.

He issued his commands on 24th October and by the 29th several crews were in open mutiny in the Wilhelmshaven dockyards. Some refused to weigh anchor. Others committed acts of sabotage or deserted outright. The mutiny was only brought under control when ships still loyal to von Hipper trained their guns on the mutineers.

Within a couple of days the mutiny had spread to Kiel. Now the sailors, joined by dockworkers, were not just refusing to serve but were demanding an end to the war. 'Frieden und brot' – 'Peace and bread' – was their slogan. The authorities responded by shooting seven of them dead. In response the mutiny grew. Many soldiers sent to stop them switched sides and joined the mutineers instead. The head of the base was forced to disguise himself and flee, as the mutineers formed their own communist councils and declared revolution.

The cry of 'Frieden und brot' spread, with communist revolts breaking out in Hamburg, Munich, Bremen and Lubeck all in early November. Germany was becoming ungovernable – and looked to be about to share the fate of Imperial Russia...

THE ROAD TO PEACE.

General Erich von Ludendorff had been seeing a psychiatrist on the advice of his staff since August 1918. He was prone to bursting into tears while in meetings with them. On 28th September he had a complete nervous breakdown while attending his headquarters. When he had recovered sufficiently, he went to see his superior Hindenburg and told him that the war must stop. Hindenburg agreed.

The next day, the two men attended a hastily arranged meeting with the Kaiser. The Kaiser accepted their views and agreed that an armistice was required. The parlous state of the German war effort was officially announced to Germany's politicians on 2nd October, much to the

Admiral Reinhard Scheer.

Men of U.S. 64th Regiment, 7th Infantry Division, celebrate the news of the **Armistice, November 11.**

Photograph taken in the forest of Compiègne after reaching an agreement for the Armistice that ended World War I. Ferdinand Foch is second from the right.

surprise of many who had no idea things were so bad.

By 4th October, the Germans were putting out feelers via the Swiss to America for peace talks. They hoped they'd get a better deal from the Americans than they would from the other Allies. Woodrow Wilson disappointed them. By 23rd October, in a united front, Allied leaders were telling the Germans that there could be no hope of peace while the current military leaders were still in place – and they were not interested in peace talks. They were only interested in surrender. Ludendorff had another near mental breakdown, decided that there was hope if Germany fought on after all and started ranting about betrayal. The Kaiser sacked him, opening up a deep and lasting wound between Germany's political and military elites. Shortly after, Ludendorff would put on a false beard and glasses and run off to Sweden.

On 5th November, President Wilson told the Germans they would have to negotiate with the Supreme Allied Commander Marshal Ferdinand Foch and no one else. It was what they had feared the most. Three days later, at Compiègne, a German peace delegation was presented with the Allied terms for surrender. They were harsh and uncompromising. Foch gave them just 72 hours to take it or leave it and rejected the German plea for an immediate ceasefire.

The war was effectively over. The German delegation was told to accept any terms in a secret coded communique from Berlin – which the Allies broke. They finally signed the agreement at 5.10am on the morning of 11th November 1918.

When the terms of surrender were disclosed, the German Imperial government collapsed and was replaced by a new German Republic headed by Friedrich Ebert. The Kaiser had already fled to Holland prior to the signing off the armistice, afraid for his own life. Once in a place of safety, he abdicated.

THE DYING DAYS

Although it had been a fairly open secret – especially amongst Allied commanders – that the Germans had sued for peace, the fighting continued.

On 10th November, the day before the Armistice, the war was still in full flow. French and American forces crossed the Meuse, stormed Hirson, and advanced towards Montmedy. British and Canadian forces were in action around Mons, ironically the site of the BEF's very first battle in 1914.

On the very last day of the war, the necessary papers were signed to stop the conflict by 5.10am. News reached civilians in London by 5.40am and Big Ben rang out for the first time since the commencement of hostilities. Gas lamps were lit in celebration in Paris. The war would officially end at 11am Paris time that day. Of course, there were still plenty of opportunities to get killed before 11.00am on 11th November. It's been estimated that some 11,000 other soldiers were killed or wounded that day – a casualty toll greater than that of D-Day.

General Pershing was in a particularly foul mood. He'd dreamed of a victory parade through the streets of Berlin itself but the armies were still entangled in France and Belgium. Peeved and looking for an opportunity to teach the Germans one final lesson, Pershing launched a number of attacks on the morning of the 11th - one as late as 10.30am - knowing full well that the war was over and won. American losses that morning were as high as 3,500 men in total. That's probably why it was an American soldier – Private Henry Gunther - who is recorded as the last Allied serviceman to die in the war, shot dead while storming a German machine gun position at 10.59am.

Artillery batteries also kept shelling their respective enemies, long after there was any point. It was discovered later that a number of men on both sides had wanted to claim the dubious distinction of having fired the last shot of the war. Other units fired off their shells just to avoid the arduous task of hauling them back home again.

The last British soldier to die in the Great War was 40-year-old Private George Ellison of the 5th Royal Irish Lancers, a professional soldier from Leeds who had been fighting on the Western Front since the outbreak of hostilities in 1914. At 9.30 in the morning of 11th November 1918, he was scouting a wood on the outskirts of Mons for signs of German activity when he was shot dead. Just 90 minutes later, the ceasefire came into effect. He was survived by his wife and 4-year-old son.

The last French soldier to die was Augustin Trébuchon. He died on the Meuse at 10.45 am, running with a message to tell his unit that hot soup would be served after the armistice.

The last Dominion soldier to die was a Canadian, George Price. His unit was still in action that morning, clearing the village of Ville sur Haine of occupying Germans and he was shot by a sniper just two minutes before the armistice. Today, there's a memorial plaque to him in the village, and a local bridge has been named in his honour.

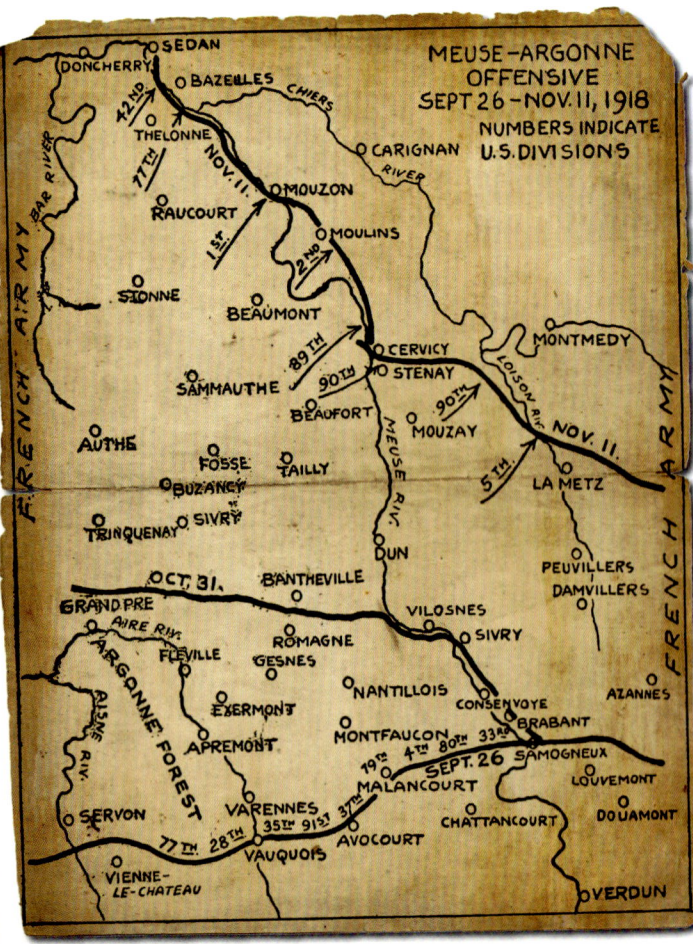

Map of battle lines and identifiers for the American divisions involved in the **Meuse-Argonne offensive** from **September 26 - November 11.** ABOVE: Map of the **Moselle-Meuse** frontier fortifications in 1914.

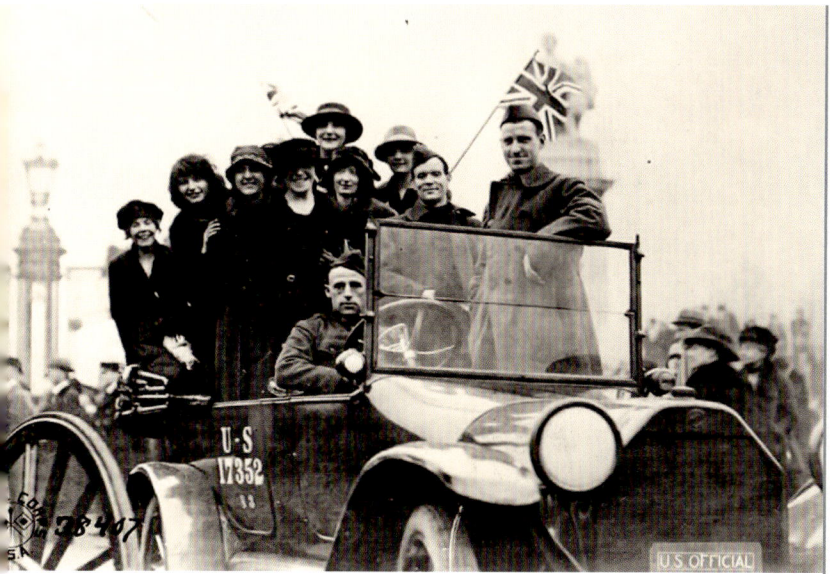

Armistice Day Celebrations, **London, 11 November 1918.**

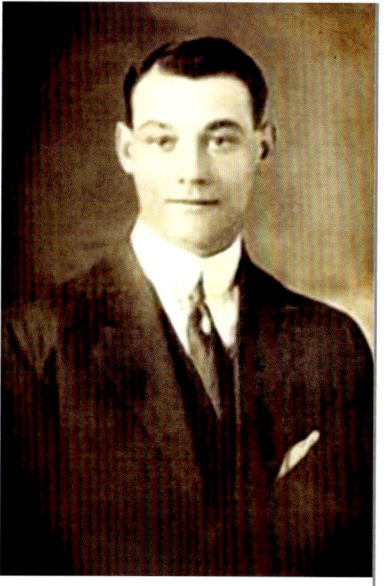

Canadian **George Lawrence Price,** the last British Empire soldier to be killed on **11th November.**

The Germans suffered 4,100 casualties on just that final morning. The last German soldier to die has never been properly established. It's generally believed to have been a German officer called Lieutenant Tomas, who approached an American unit to tell them that the war was over...

These are the official 'last deaths' but in truth, the killing went on for many hours on the Western Front after the armistice amid the last chaotic thrashings of the war.

At an Allied field hospital near Etaples, the wards were adorned with a simple notice:

'To celebrate the conclusion of hostilities every patient will be allowed an extra piece of bread and jam with his tea.'

"All the News That's Fit to Print."

The New York Times.

THE WEATHER

NEW YORK, MONDAY, NOVEMBER 11, 1918. TWENTY-FOUR PAGES

ARMISTICE SIGNED, END OF THE WAR!
BERLIN SEIZED BY REVOLUTIONISTS;
NEW CHANCELLOR BEGS FOR ORDER;
OUSTED KAISER FLEES TO HOLLAND

SON FLEES WITH EX-KAISER | Kaiser Fought Hindenburg's Call for Abdication; Failed to Get Army's Support in Keeping Throne | BERLIN TROOPS JOIN REVOLT | Socialist Chancellor Appeals to All Germans To Help Him Save Fatherland from Anarchy | WAR ENDS AT 6 O'CLOCK THIS MORNING

PEACE
WORLD WAR ENDS AS GERMANY SIGNS ARMISTICE!

HUNS QUIT!

WHOLE COUNTRY CELEBRATING
TERMS OF ARMISTICE ANNOUNCED TODAY
Terms of Armistice Strips Germany of all Conquered Territory; and Restoration of Devastated Lands; Naval Units Surrender and Army Demobilizes

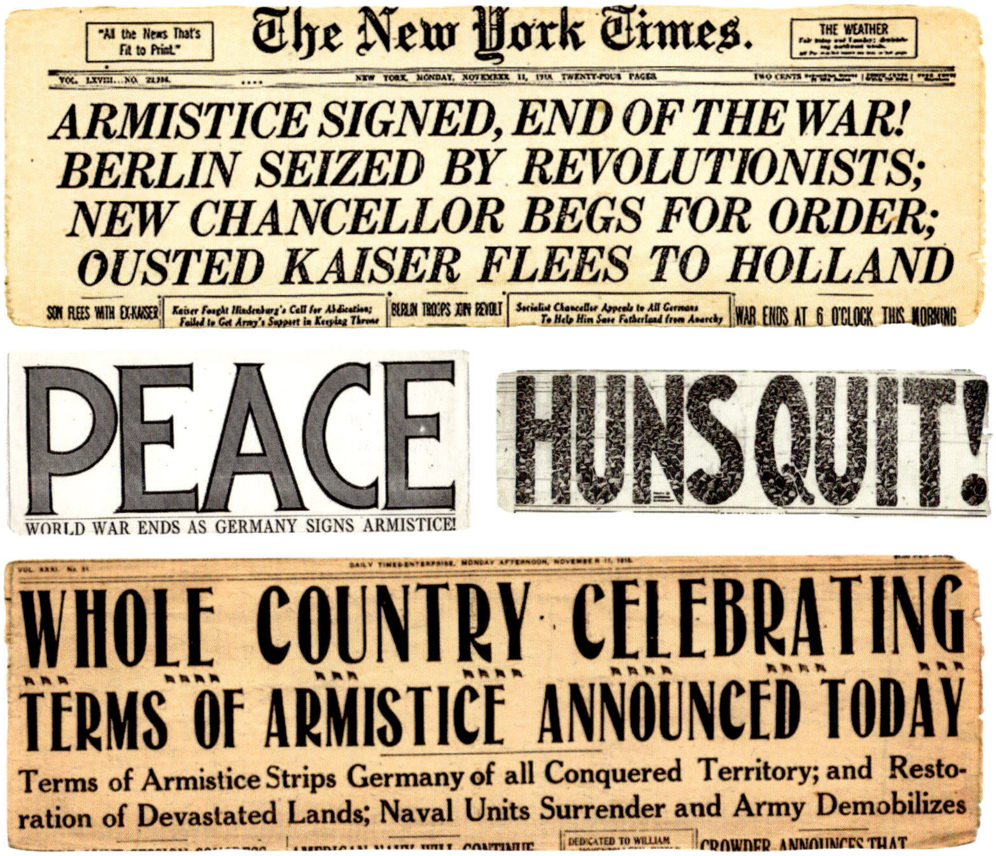

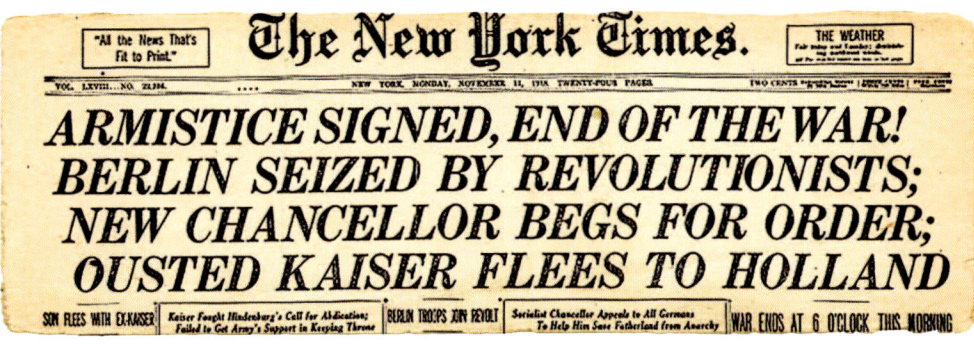

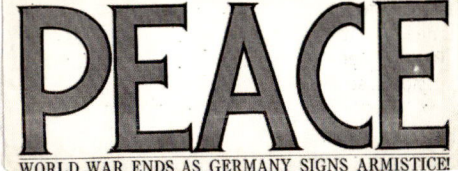

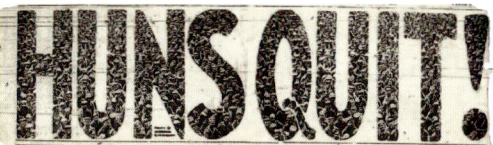

A collection of Newspaper clippings reporting the end.

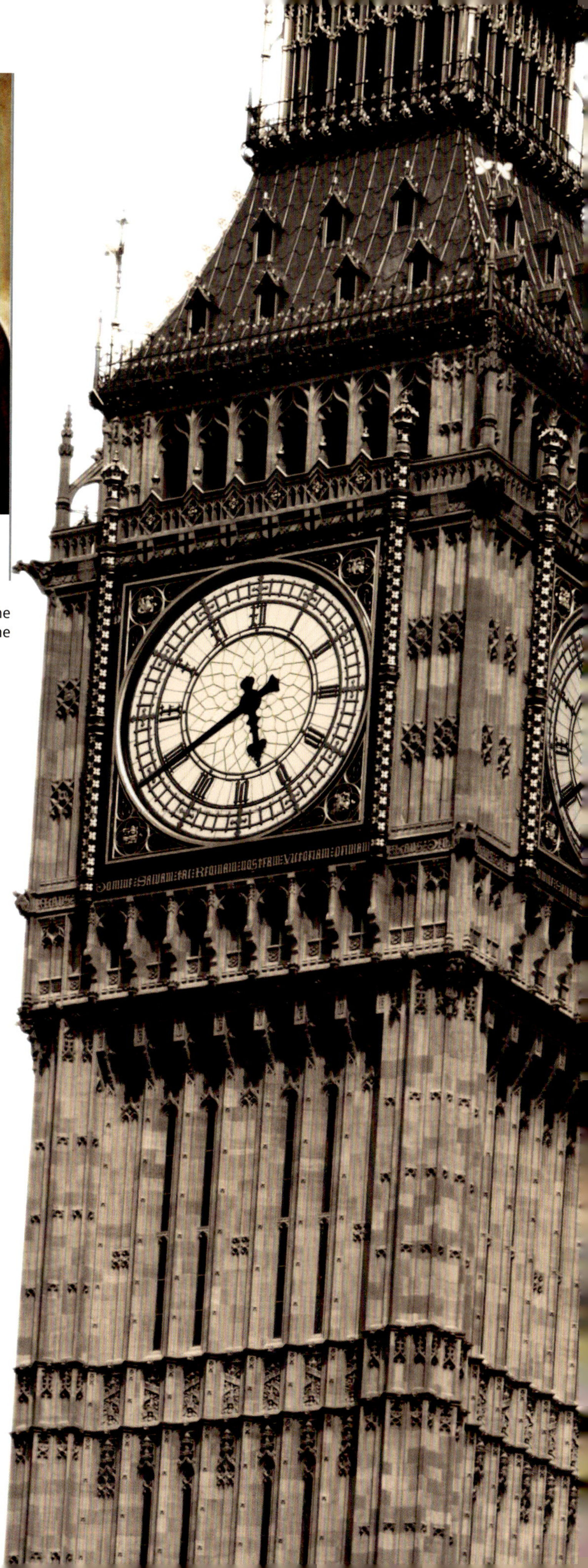

"First to Fight": A group of U.S. Marines pose for recruiting shot.

American soldiers going into action, Badouville March 1918.

Gun crew from Regimental Headquarters Company, 23rd Infantry, firing 37mm gun during an advance against German entrenched positions

A German CL.IIIa airplane brought down in the Forest of Argonne by American machine gunners between Montfaucon and Cierges, 4 October 1918.

German machine gunners lie died after trying to stop an Australian advance Near Estrees, October 1918.

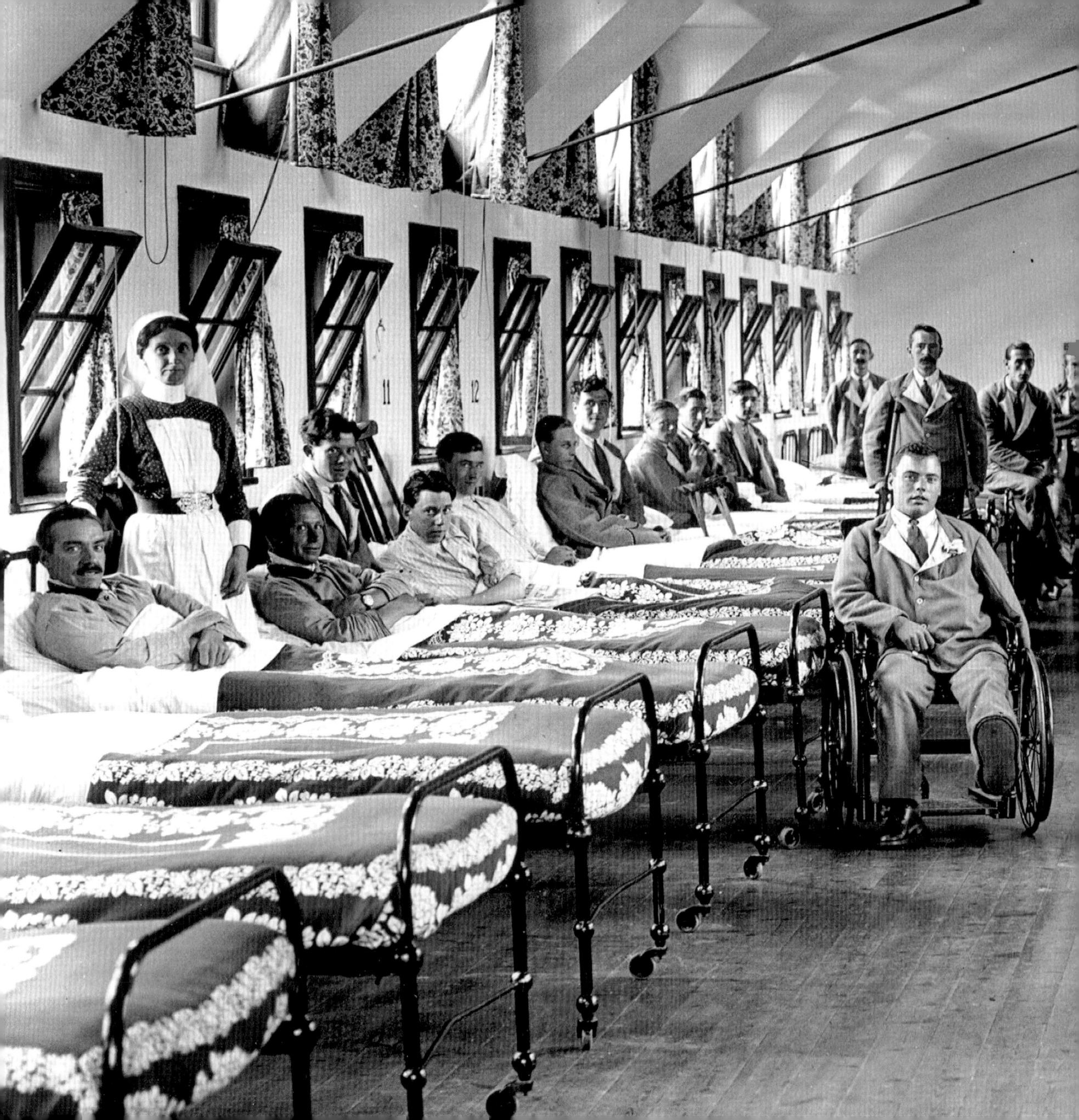

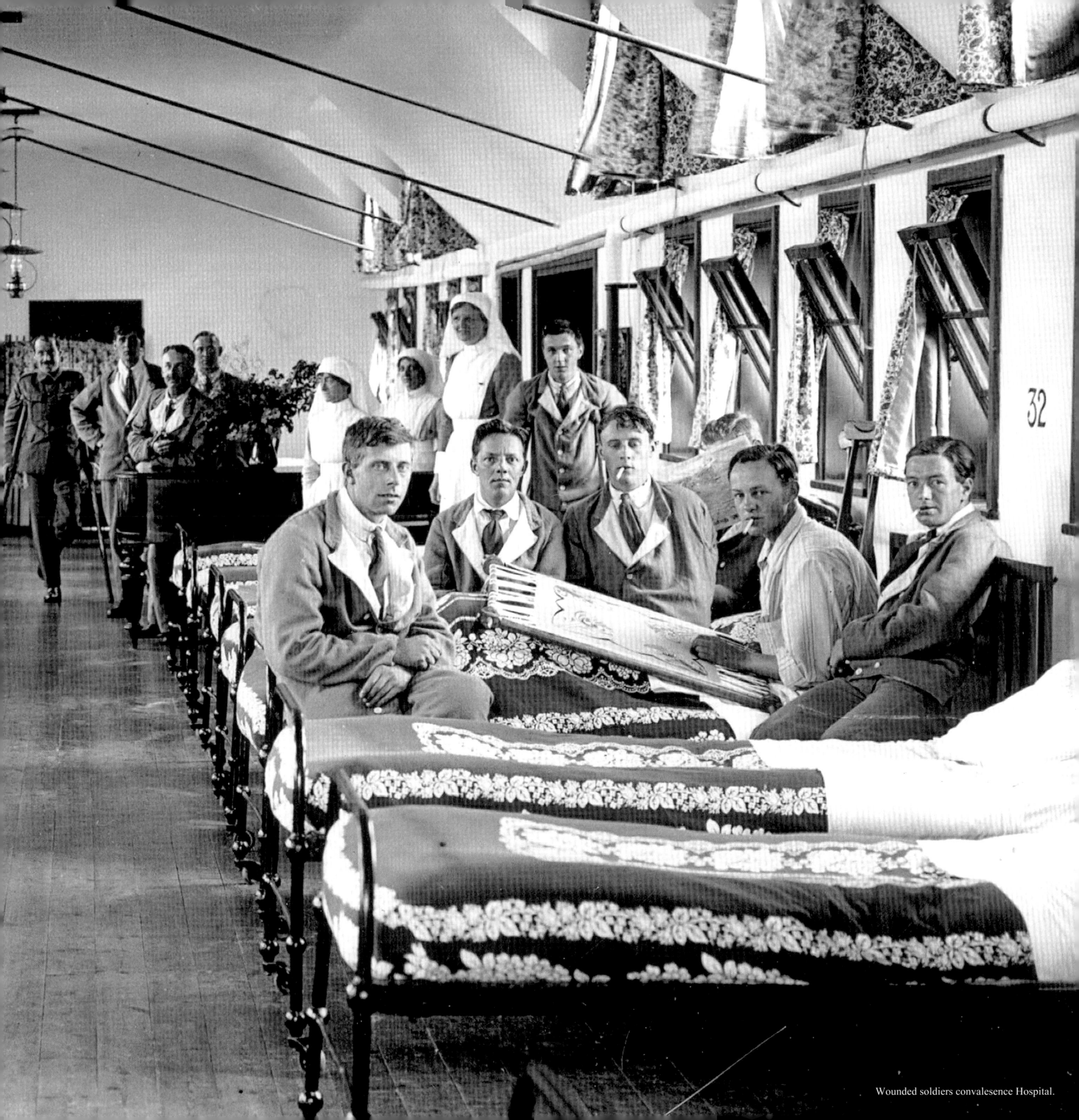

Wounded soldiers convalesence Hospital.

The crowd surging around Versailles Palace after the signing of the treaty, June 28, 1919.

After the signing, **President Woodrow Wilson** in the center of the photo with top hat.

The Signing of the Peace Treaty in the Hall of Mirrors, Versailles 1919 by William Orpen.

Placard for Lloyd's News, announcing the signing of the **Treaty of Versailles.**

VERSAILLES AND BEYOND

After three months of talks, the Great War was finally concluded at Versailles on 28th June 1919. The talks were between the leaders of the victorious Allied powers and no Germans were consulted until the final weeks, when they were given an ultimatum – sign the treaty or be invaded. It took so long because the various Allied leaders wanted different things out of the peace treaty.

Georges Clemenceau, Prime Minister of France and nick-named 'The Tiger', wanted raw and bloody revenge against the Germans. He wanted Germany smashed, crippled and left in no state ever to rise up and start a war again. Although the British public were demanding pretty much the same thing, with cries of 'Hang the Kaiser!' Prime Minister Lloyd George had secret worries about demolishing the German nation. Since the Russian Revolution of 1917, he had been very fearful of the rise of international communism. If Germany was punished too severely, he thought, communism might take strong root there. If a diminished Germany could still stand, it might be a useful buffer against the communists. President Wilson just wanted to wash his hands of the whole thing, pacify Europe and get back to America being isolationist. And no one cared what the Italians wanted.

The eventual treaty was a compromise – harsh but not the equivalent of a death sentence for the German nation. Germany's army was limited, her navy reduced to six ships (and no submarines) and she was forbidden to have tanks or an air force. Germany also had to give up a number of territories and sign Clause 231 - the 'War Guilt Clause'. Signing this meant that Germany accepted the blame for the Great War and agreed to pay damages to the victorious nations.

The German public and the German military were furious about the terms. Those who signed the treaty were to become known as the 'November Criminals'. The German military in particular believed that they had not lost the war - but had been stabbed in the back by treacherous politicians and 'special business interests' (read: The Jews). The nation festered with resentment, fractured between communist and fascist radicals, collapsed and eventually re-militarised.

The treaty also led to Wilson's dream of the 'League of Nations', a forerunner of the United Nations, which was intended to maintain world peace. Strangely, Germany was excluded from joining and The League of Nations failed utterly. The horrors of the Great War haunted the politicians of the era and, when Germany rose again, they did everything they could to appease its Nazi leaders and to prevent a second war. They simply could not understand – or did not want to consider - that German national pride demanded a re-run of the war. More than sixty million men, women and children died as a result.

Britain lost 750,000 men in the Great War. A further million and a half were wounded. France suffered almost 1,500,000 men dead. Germany had mourned two million men. Beyond that, whole empires fell. The new German Empire died almost before it had been born. The Austro-Hungarian Empire collapsed in ruins. Imperial Russia fell to the Communists and the old Ottoman Empire of the Turks finally crumbled too. New nations rose from the ruins – Poland and Czechoslovakia among them. America, almost against its will, became a leading force in the world.

People changed too, hardened by war. In Britain, the soldiers were not prepared to return to a world of crippling low pay, grinding poverty and forelock tugging to their betters. The women, many of whom had served the war effort at the Home Front, were granted near-universal suffrage and felt capable of achieving so much more in their lives than they did during that long languid summer of Edwardian England.

The world produced radically new art and music. Hemlines rose. The Twenties roared and shook off the last vestiges of Victoriana. Above all there was a new sense of freedom and of the individual. The war had ushered in a new modern age and altered the very mind of man.

As Joe Young and Sam M. Lewis wrote prophetically in 1918,

'How you gonna keep 'em down on the farm, after they've seen Paree?'